MILITARY POWER

NUCLEAR FIRST USE

MILITARY POWER

A series produced in conjunction with
The Royal United Services Institute for Defence Studies

GENERAL EDITOR GROUP CAPTAIN DAVID BOLTON.
RAF (Ret)
EDITOR DR BRIAN HOLDEN REID

In the highly dangerous world in which we live, the subject of defence, and of all kinds of warfare, becomes increasingly relevant in day-to-day life. These studies – concise, topical, well written, meticulously balanced, and reasonably priced – not only provide the reader with background information, but also offer a platform for differing but expert views. Each book carries an introduction by an eminent figure, and is aimed at the general reader as well as at those with a professional interest.

MILITARY POWER

NUCLEAR FIRST USE

NEVILLE BROWN
and
ANTHONY FARRAR-HOCKLEY

THE ROYAL UNITED SERVICES
INSTITUTE FOR DEFENCE STUDIES

BUCHAN & ENRIGHT, PUBLISHERS,
LONDON

First published in 1985 by
Buchan & Enright, Publishers, Limited
53 Fleet Street, London EC4Y 1BE

British Library Cataloguing in Publication Data

Brown, Neville
Nuclear first use. – (Military Power)
1. No first use (Nuclear Strategy)
I. Title   II. Farrar-Hockley, Sir Anthony
III. Series
355'.0217   U264

ISBN 0-907675-26-3

Photoset in North Wales by
Derek Doyle & Associates, Mold, Clwyd
Printed in Great Britain at
The Pitman Press, Bath

CONTENTS

Abbreviations 6

Preface   David Bolton 7

PART I   ASPECTS OF DETERRENCE:
A COMMAND PERSPECTIVE 9

PART II   NUCLEAR FIRST USE: AN OVERVIEW   21

1   Deterrence In Europe 23

2   The Control of Escalation 38

3   The Changing Face of War 153

4   The Central European Theatre 73

5   The Wider Compass 83

6   Towards A Broader Consensus? 90

Notes and References 104

Index 107

ABBREVIATIONS

ABM	ANTI-BALLISTIC MISSILE
ASW	ANTI-SUBMARINE WARFARE
BMD	BALLISTIC MISSILE DEFENCE
CINCCHAN	COMMANDER-IN-CHIEF CHANNEL
CND	CAMPAIGN FOR NUCLEAR DISARMAMENT
COMECON	COUNCIL FOR MUTUAL ECONOMIC ASSISTANCE
FBM	FLEET BALLISTIC MISSILES
GFSG	GROUND FORCES SOVIET GERMANY
GLCM	GROUND-LAUNCHED CRUISE MISSILES
ICBM	INTERCONTINENTAL BALLISTIC MISSILES
IRBM	INTERMEDIATE-RANGE BALLISTIC MISSILES
MAD	MUTUAL ASSURED DESTRUCTION
MRBM	MEDIUM-RANGE BALLISTIC MISSILES
NPG	NUCLEAR PLANNING GROUP
PGM	PRECISION GUIDED MUNITIONS
RDJTF	RAPID DEPLOYMENT JOINT TASK FORCE
SACEUR	SUPREME ALLIED COMMANDER EUROPE
SACLANT	SUPREME ALLIED COMMANDER ATLANTIC
SALT-1	STRATEGIC ARMS LIMITATION TALKS
SDR	SPECIAL DRAWING RIGHTS
SLBM	SUBMARINE-LAUNCHED BALLISTIC MISSILES

PREFACE

BY GROUP CAPTAIN DAVID BOLTON
DIRECTOR RUSI

Founded in 1831 with the Duke of Wellington as its first president, the Royal United Services Institute for Defence Studies has operated since 1860 under Royal Charter charged with examining the full range of questions related to the military sciences. The RUSI is a fully independent body but its membership largely comprises those with authority and responsibility, coupled with practical good sense, within their own particular field. In addition to being the professional Institute of the Armed Forces, the RUSI's membership includes those from industry and academe, the media, civil servants and parliamentarians, as well as the military. The Institute therefore acts as a bridge between different constituencies and disciplines concerned with defence by drawing on the diverse interests and responsibilities of its members. The RUSI further seeks to enhance informed opinion and to encourage a wider understanding and debate of important defence issues. In this, the Military Power Series is designed to play an important part by questioning and helping to formulate ideas on topical subjects of the moment.

Deterrence is very much a matter of perception. To be effective, a potential aggressor must perceive that the risk and potential cost of a prospective military attack are too high, no matter what the political ends. There are many components in this equation: military capability, readiness and efficiency, political will and resolution, are just some of these. However, in practical terms, it is the correlation between nuclear and conventional forces, particularly in the European theatre, which is central to deterrence theory. The ratio between nuclear and conventional forces, both within the Atlantic Alliance and between NATO and the Warsaw Pact, is of particular relevance today when there are calls for a policy of 'no-first-use' of nuclear weapons or, at least, of no early use of those weapons in any future conflict. Serious doubts are also being raised as to the value of a policy of nuclear deterrence which, if it failed, would result in the mutual destruction of the protagonists. To counter-balance this public concern, as well as military doubts, there are now increasing efforts to promote 'conventional deterrence' thereby further reducing dependence upon nuclear weapons. All these arguments impinge upon any discussion of concepts of operations, arms control negotiations, and the military utility of new technologies. These and many related questions are addressed in this book by Professor Neville Brown, a noted authority on matters of strategic affairs and international relations, and General Sir Anthony Farrar-Hockley, a leading author and military historian as well as a commander of international repute and therefore a practitioner of the military sciences.

Defence questions and, in particular, nuclear issues, give rise to strong emotion. Rational argument provides a better response and a firmer basis of knowledge. It is the perception of realities, as opposed to popular myth and emotion, which has also long promoted the work of the RUSI and it is similarly consonant both with the aims of this book and the whole Military Power Series.

In any democratic society, public understanding and support are fundamental to sustaining a viable policy for the security of essential freedoms and interests. It is hoped that an objective perspective will be provided in this book and its successors to further public interest and awareness.

Part I

Aspects of Deterrence:
A Command Perspective

BY GENERAL SIR ANTHONY FARRAR-HOCKLEY

ASPECTS OF DETERRENCE: A COMMAND PERSPECTIVE

Public knowledge concerning what NATO is and does is noticeably slight. Important though it is acknowledged to be, defence does not command widespread attention and the disinformation services of the Soviet Union, anxieties concerning the dreadful power of nuclear weapons, and intermittent political and occasional military schism within the Atlantic Alliance have combined over the past 30 years to obscure the abiding service of the North Atlantic Treaty Organisation as a whole to peace and stability. The attempts of member governments to remedy this from time to time have been no more than marginally successful as, almost inevitably, their efforts have been delivered in packages attractive only to *aficionados* of defence. With some important exceptions, journalists in press, radio and television are interested in NATO events only if they can be represented as spectacular or scandalous.

Yet every now and again the issues that divide east and west in Europe and beyond come to the boil and there are indications that they are currently simmering. This is not to say that the various anti-nuclear movements are at last winning the propaganda war; they continue, if anything, to confuse the debate. The recent US Presidential election has certainly added heat to the discussion but continually rising costs and concomitant budgetary pressures are probably the main elements persuading government ministers that some changes in defence policy must be made.

They will not be short of advice as they look at policy options. High officials and officers charged with responsibility for implementing policy will ensure that they are aware of the threats to security and counsel measures which will minimise risks to as great an extent as possible. Both inside and outside the apparatus of government, lobbyists on the right will urge the necessity of massive military superiority for NATO over the USSR. The technology camp will point to the potential of the West to outstrip its opponents in fielding new weapons or equipment systems while some of its extreme enthusiasts may even propose that all supply funds should be devoted to making a quantum jump ahead of the USSR. The clamour to ban the bomb will be intensified. The more reasoned voices advocating 'no first use' or 'no weapons that suggest aggression' will be lifted up. So, where do we stand? Who should we heed?

Two crucial considerations continually weigh upon the three chief NATO commanders, SACEUR, SACLANT and CINCCHAN, as they regard their directives. The first is that the organisation each serves is wedded essentially to a defensive strategy. Whilst this is no doubt uplifting in the moral sense, the practical consequence is that, if war comes, each will lack surprise and hence the initative. As the Soviet Union dominates the Warsaw Pact, it will have choice of time, place, thrust lines and hence the opportunity to maximise the impact of its strikes by sea, land and air forces at the outset. In contrast, NATO forces will be obliged to respond by manning all the frontiers until the main thrusts are identified; not an easy task as some apparently threatening concentrations will be simulated by advanced methods of deception. Redeployment to meet those materialising then has to be undertaken under conditions of perilous disadvantage.

Such a statement of the simple facts should not suggest that the forces of the Warsaw Pact will take NATO territory completely by surprise on, say, one sunny Sunday afternoon in June when the vedettes are lightly manned and the supporting garrisons are asleep or at play. That is a possibility but now a remote one. The North Koreans attacked South Korea in such a manner in 1950 with complete surprise. They had massed two corps secretly along the frontier in full possession of first and second line ammunition, fuel and rations. A long term policy of ruthlessly constraining the movement of the civil population had denied the passing of anything but fragmentary reports of troop concentrations to the south. All instructions for planning and operational deployment were carried to respective headquarters by hand of officer; nothing passed by radio or telephone on these matters. But technical intelligence today is much advanced on that available in 1950. It is thus assumed that the surprise attack *tout simple* is unlikely.

Surprise may still be attainable by an aggressor, however, where it is possible to put forces into the field ahead of the defence, even though the defending parties may be aware of the intention. The Warsaw Pact forces are effectively within a single Russian political and military command system. Various arrangements can be made thereby to mobilise and deploy speedily. Final concentrations will almost certainly be detected prior to the launch of hostilities and, similarly, such essential functions as the breaking out of ammunition cannot easily be disguised; huge quantities are involved and the expense of keeping the range of operational ammunition dispersed in small packets outside magazines for any period would be prohibitive. The NATO governments and their military commands would therefore begin to receive warnings of impending attack; progressive and cumulative warnings. As a command organisation which has fifteen heads, however, (including France, Spain and Portugal) it has the problem of obtaining early common agreement as to the import of these warnings. In 1973, the Israeli government, possessed of a not inconsiderable technical intelligence among a number of resources and enjoying a high expertise in this function overall, was taken by surprise because, as they frankly admitted when they studied their errors post-war, they preferred not to heed the information offered them. Given substantive evidence of mobilisation and deployment to attack stations by the Warsaw Pact, there is an immediate requirement of the NATO governments to mobilise themselves. Collective mobilisation by the membership as a response to that of the Warsaw Pact forces is the last act of deterrence available to the Atlantic Alliance; but there is a likelihood that this will not immediately be a common perception among political leaders confronted by the prospect of a Third World War. Some political and perhaps military counsellors may advise that mobilisation will be a form of provocation and suggest that it would be better to wait for the commission of an act of war before making a decision. Financial counsellors may remind cabinets of the expense of fruitless mobilisation. The clock would tick on through precious wasted hours if such counsels prevailed while the NATO commanders were denied the essential reinforcement of their standing forces and the intermediate alert measures requiring ministerial authority remained in suspense. Hesitation, procrastination, the attributes of politico-military command by committee, enable a single-minded aggressor, acting in full view, to effect surprise.

The other major disadvantage inherent in NATO's essentially defensive strategy is the comparative weakness of its forces *vis-à-vis* those of the Warsaw Pact. The latter is overwhelmingly stronger, a fact obscured in a sense by the frequent manifestation of the numbers of men available in sea, land and air commands, warships, tanks, guns, missile launchers, aircraft. These indicate a disparity but not one so great as to cause the general reader's cheeks to go ashen if he depends upon the NATO umbrella to keep him dry. Indeed, in one or two fields – strategic nuclear weaponry, for example – a degree of superiority falls to NATO. What is not manifest is the capability of the Warsaw Pact forces for sustained combat. Its trained manpower exceeds that of NATO by two million. Its conventional ammunition stocks exceed those of NATO by a factor of ten and include an element almost abandoned by NATO, chemical weapons, specifically, nerve droplets. Its stocks of replacement weapons and equipment exceed those of NATO by a factor of five.

The capacity of the Warsaw Pact forces to accept casualties, yet to sustain mobile offensive sea and air, land and air operations is therefore considerable; that of NATO relatively poor. The frequently expressed view that the latter's capability to sustain a conventional defence is limited to a matter of days is not an exaggeration of weakness; it is probable that in a completely conventional war NATO would run out of weapons platforms, munitions, and certain essential items of equipment before it altogether ran out of fighting men.

Possession of chemical weapons enhances this superiority. At present, substantial numbers of NATO forces either lack entirely the special clothing and equipment needed to protect them against nerve agents or certain items essential to full protection. This may be in part due to the fact that surprisingly little is said about the threat from chemical attack; in some of the member states it was until very recently thought impolitic to mention the subject and thus there was a corresponding lack of political will to admit that any pressing need arose for provision. All the European members of the Atlantic Alliance have abandoned voluntarily any capacity, if they had it, for chemical warfare and so has Canada. Long since, the United States ceased manufacturing shells and aircraft dispensers but possesses a dwindling stock of these – dwindling because they are ageing and year by year more items among them have to be destroyed. The Soviet Union was among those nations which condemned chemical warfare but it declined to sign any protocol obliging it to eschew manufacture or retention of existing stocks. Indeed, as others stopped manufacture or altogether rid themselves of such weapons, the Soviet high command developed its own capability to wage chemical warfare by surface and air delivery, and currently has a flourishing chemical weapons industry. It is remarkable that, as the United States has proposed to modernise its own means of delivering nerve agents in war, the Soviet Union has expressed interest in controlling such weapons.

Comprehending only the very limited United States capability, a NATO view has developed that the use of chemical weapons against its peoples, civil or military, would be sufficiently serious to warrant a tactical nuclear response; and some who hold that opinion have suggested that it would be wise to inform the USSR of it in advance so as to deter any such attack. The operational doctrine manifest in the training publications and practice of the Red Army suggests that quite a different point of view is held by its policy makers. Their concept of war embraces the use of all and any weapons likely to show at the time of use an overall advantage to the particular commander and those whom he serves. Chemical weapons are simulated in every major exercise conducted by the land forces of the Soviet Union. It is notable that the specialist cleansing squads which follow up a strike occupy themselves solely in decontaminating enemy areas. There is no expectation of a chemical attack upon their own territory.

This discussion brings into view the matter of nuclear warfare. The foregoing has been concerned principally with conventional operations. Despite the prognostications of the anti-nuclear lobby, it is unlikely, as Professor Brown remarks, that the opening of a Third World War would involve an immediate nuclear holocaust on the initiative of either side. The retention of conventional armed forces, at least to the extent of current numbers and armament, would be pointless if such was the intention. The NATO policy is that it reserves to itself the moment to decide if and when it will embark on the nuclear ladder. There is no specific plan to launch a nuclear weapon; only to be ready to do so if circumstances warrant it. Such circumstances might arise, for example, if the Supreme Allied Commander, Europe – SACEUR – found that his forces were no longer capable of resisting the conventional pressure of the enemy. It would then be his duty to inform the heads of governments that defeat would follow within a matter of hours unless he had authority to use one or more tactical nuclear weapons. The governments would either agree to their use or deny them. If battlefield nuclear weapons were used, it is conceivable that fighting might thereby come to an end after a brief exchange. Much would depend upon the price the Soviet Union was prepared to pay for its objectives.

This is a NATO scenario. The Soviet concept, as manifested in respect of chemical weapons, does not make such fine distinctions. There has been, however, in recent years a tendency to accept that the penalties of using nuclear weapons on the battlefield as simply one element of the offensive are so wide ranging as to necessitate special rules for their use; but there is still a strong faction in the high command which regards this as dangerously restrictive. The possibility must thus be accepted that the opening of a Soviet offensive might at once or shortly thereafter involve an inceptory nuclear strike as well as the use of one or more chemical weapons, particularly if there were indications of irresolution or dissension among the NATO membership concerning the use of their own tactical nuclear weapons.

The inception of nuclear or chemical warfare would, of course, be a deliberate act of policy by the Soviet Union rather than one of purely military expedience. Whatever uncertainties disturb the outside world concerning the might of the Warsaw Pact or the uses to which this may be put, none arise as to the arrangements for and validity of the central control of nuclear and, initially, chemical weapon launches. Curiously, any doubts about control in the western world relate to the NATO system: to the fire control discipline in the silo batteries, the submarine rocketry, the land based tactical missiles such as Cruise and Pershing, the artillery shells and atomic mines under United States command; and on the periphery of power those of the United Kingdom and France.

Ignorance of or disbelief in the efficacy of the systems controlling these weapons feeds the anxiety of those outside the security fences who, from time to time, contemplate the dreadful prospect of a nuclear war. Anxiety is stimulated further by the verisimilitudinous revelations of journalists or the imagination of playwrights and novelists: Dr Strangelove is ever with us, either in his own persona or that of a mad president or maniacal general bent on starting a nuclear war. A fondness for hyperbole in the defence field in the United States is not helpful in exposure of the absurdity of these images. For the sake of variety, they are transformed now and again into subordinate figures: the submarine commander discovered at some ocean depth with a shaking hand whose unsteadiness causes him to misread the instructions in a signal which in turn prompts him to press a button instantly to despatch his nuclear missile load on to targets in the Soviet Union. Or again, the infantry or tank battalion commander overwrought in the battle line by seeing an overwhelming number of the enemy about to advance upon him. He orders his artillery observer to fire a nuclear shell as the only means of saving his force. Somehow, the control system for release of the weapon is circumvented and the shell is fired. The enemy force remains obligingly in position during the relatively long period required to gather and prepare the special warhead. When the shell is fired it is directed on to a target within visual range of the battalion commander and his observer – say, 3,000 metres distant at most. Its effect upon those calling for it is therefore almost as grievous as those it is intended to destroy, but this is not apparent in the unilateralist's or the pacifist's scenario. It is anyhow good material for the propaganda agencies of the Soviet Union.

Anxieties of a more realistic kind plague the NATO senior commanders and associated national military staffs. When intelligence reveals an uprating of the Warsaw Pact's capacity for aggression there is a natural wish to offset it. In the process of politico-military consultation, a number of cupboards are opened. Reopening of the nuclear cupboard may provide a further means of buttressing deterrence but it may also provide hostages to political fortunes. A safer door is that marked 'Extended Technology'. Opened, it reveals many glittering prospectuses underwritten by the record of proven superiority in science and technology in the West. What may go unremarked is the heap of earlier projects which have failed to mature. The fact is that there have been very few major advances in defence or any other field of science of technology over a short span of time; most advances have come about as the result of long development. Between the wars the Germans used product development successfully in the improvement of their main battle tanks; the Russians have followed in this path. The United States and sometimes France, the Federal Republic of Germany, Italy and the United Kingdom have made some small surges forward which have justified the expenditure involved, but as often they have wasted huge sums. This is not to suggest that members of the Atlantic Alliance should abstain from bold policies in defence research and development; simply that because resources are constrained, greater care should be exercised in the selection of objectives. Meantime, those who are looking into the cupboard for items of extended technology to provide an immediate means of compensating NATO weakness would do well to remember that the navies, armies and air forces will fight, if war is forced upon them, with the weapons, equipment and supplies actually in their possession. There are one or two items in the late stages of development which may yield important dividends at the end of this decade but with these exceptions, the NATO forces will still be equipped at the end of the century with the weapons platforms and weapons that are in service or about to come into service *now*.

This consideration should prompt those seeking to extend deterrence of war for another thirty years and more, to open the cupboard marked 'Current Inventory'. It is not quite like Mother Hubbard's but the shelves are not plentifully filled. Many promises have been made to stock up to the modest levels long agreed. Too few have been kept and the reason is well known: defence is an expensive business and getting more expensive all the time. It is not a prime vote winner, though some politicians might well now reflect upon the evidence that, treated derisively, it may be a vote loser. Fresh contributions to the Current Inventory cupboard will not be as politically hazardous as those to the nuclear shelves next door or attract as much interest as those to its Extended Technology neighbour, but they will *inter alia* emphasise the point that consistency and steadiness are more likely to reduce risks of war than continual innovation. Deterrence through an adequate defence will not be achieved by reliance on one category of weapons – nuclear or conventional – or the quantum jump which will suddenly render the Warsaw Pact defenceless. It will not be achieved by the adoption of eccentric philosophies such as unilateralism and its bedfellow, pacifism. Supporters of the latter would do well to reflect upon that inscription posted in the armour of the commonwealth of Venice in the sixteenth century: 'Happy is that city which in time of peace thinks of war'. Those who suggest lesser but yet substantive concessions to the Soviet Union in face of the evidence of its rapacious pursuit of political and military advantage – such as yielding to pressure for a 'no first use of nuclear weapons' declaration – might equally reflect with advantage upon John Hampden's dictum that 'the essence of war is violence, and that moderation in war is imbecility.'

Part II
Nuclear First Use: An Overview

BY PROFESSOR NEVILLE BROWN

CHAPTER ONE

DETERRENCE IN EUROPE

Quite apart from the death and destruction that would directly be caused, hostilities between NATO and the Warsaw Pact on any scale and for any length of time would have grim strategic, economic and political consequences for all Mankind. Yet unless one or the other of these alliances was being crippled by discord, those hostilities could not end in outright victory for either side, given the ultimate realities of nuclear overkill. So it can well be argued that the sharpest and most negative threshold of conflict escalation is not that between non-nuclear and nuclear or non-chemical and chemical. It is that between armed peace and any kind of European war. On this account alone, it is imperative that the quest for European security encompasses issues other than NATO's capability for waging armed conflict. It must also be much concerned with deterrence, arms control and political dialogue. However, this is by no means to suggest that the capability just mentioned is of small or diminishing consequence. On the contrary, it remains the most basic and tangible element in deterrence. Hence only a sufficiency of it may enable NATO and its member states to be suitably outgoing in political dialogue with their Warsaw Pact counterparts.

This being so, the cavalier fashion in which certain students of these matters have lately become converts to 'no first use' of nuclear firepower is something utterly deplored by Sir Anthony Farrar-Hockley and myself. For it is our belief that the adoption by NATO of a 'no first use' policy would be a disastrous blunder. We further believe that 'no early use' would be quite wrong if by that is meant a prior commitment to fight a non-nuclear war for many days or even weeks, regardless of how a war had started or was proceeding or even where it was taking place. Needless to say, we further think that a grave error would be seriously compounded if the Alliance publicly endorsed either precept.

Particularly do we urge political parties, religious denominations and other influential bodies within the Atlantic community never to turn to either without the most thorough deliberation. Above all, they should never do so in order that they may quickly fix a consensus within their own ranks as between the unilateral disarmers and those who are not prepared thus to weaken or destroy the military and political foundations of NATO. Nor, for that matter, should any advocates of either a one-sided or a two-sided 'nuclear freeze', whether from Europe or North America, be allowed to get away with talking about nuclear weapons in one and the same breath. For one thing, neither the qualitative nor the quantitative aspects of the theatre nuclear balance in Europe correspond to those of the strategic nuclear balance between the Superpowers. The former is bound never to be as stable operationally as the latter has become (see Chapter 3). Added to which, the presence of US nuclear warheads in the European theatre contributes in a special way to political reassurance. The two dimensions complement each other in the preservation of deterrence, in respect of the European continent and the maritime approaches thereto.

The need to approach with caution the possibility of any very drastic changes in NATO's philosophy of nuclear defence is made all the more compelling by a marked subjectiveness in military science; the terminological inexactitude of this discipline; the hazards of predicting changes in technology and their operational impact; and the confused nature of the historical record. To take terminology first, it has to be said that just about the most inappropriate and constrictive usage in this whole field is one which bears directly on the debate about nuclear first use. The allusion is to 'conventional' war, forces, weapons and so on. The genesis of this malapropism lay, of course, in the search for an adjective able to embrace the notion of set-piece though non-nuclear contests between regular (in contrast with guerilla) forces. Yet it is likewise employed when referring to elements that do also have relevance to theatre nuclear conflict, either in the sense that they could actually release nuclear warheads or because they could perform other roles germane to a nuclear environment. When he was US Secretary of Defense (1960-8), Robert McNamara preferred to use the term 'general purpose' when making reference to such systems or units. But the precedent he tried to set was never widely followed.

These days, the most serious objection to this word 'conventional' is the way it conjures up images of warfare in the Western Desert and so on, 40 years ago. Alas, the multiple and ever-accelerating revolution in electronics is alone enough to ensure that, 10 to 15 years hence, even a non-nuclear conflict waged across central Europe would bear no more resemblance to the great battles of World War Two than did they to those of 1914-18. Nor may our collective recollection of those previous eras correspond at all closely with historical reality. For instance, we tend to see the Western Desert as an arena in which agile formations of 'cruiser' tanks manoeuvred freely and endlessly: the 'fleets on land' ideal of the classic armoured theorists. Yet the plain fact is that the three critical battles of 1942 (Gazala, Alam Halfa and Alamein) were shaped by vast belts of minefields, while the decisive factor in Wavell's famous surge through Cyrenaica in the winter of 1940-1 had been his use of slow but very solid 'infantry' tanks to reduce Italian strongpoints along the coast.[1] Besides, whatever may appear to be the military probabilities as stated in general terms, the history of warfare, not least that of World War Two, is laced with examples of surprising victories or else surprising avoidance of defeat. Admittedly, this subject is a hard one to summarize because history is always untidy and because prior expectations are never easy to gauge in retrospect and will, in any case, always be ambiguous and diverse. But among many episodes in 1939 and 1940 that worked out a lot differently from what many analysts had anticipated must surely be numbered the following: the Russian invasion of Finland; the German invasion of Norway; the fall of France; the evacuation from Dunkirk; the Battle of Britain; the Italian invasion of Greece; and the Wavell Desert offensive. Enough here alone, one might have thought, to warn anybody off foreclosing, explicitly and absolutely, such an option as the early use of the most potent weapons in one's armoury.

Moreover, the claims of prudence become yet stronger as one examines the case for NATO as such avowedly committing itself to 'no first use' of nuclear weapons. For what with the inertia inherent in multi-national bureaucracies and with all the emotions and anxieties engendered by the whole question of nuclear weapons, it could prove appallingly difficult ever to disavow such a pledge once it had become enshrined in Alliance doctrine. What is more, the difficulty would be compounded by the insistence of its supporters that 'no first use' represented a superior moral stance. Therefore, the leadership of NATO might be obliged to persevere with such a precept in the face of advances in military technology far beyond those currently in train and so that much harder to evaluate, either now or later. It would also have to be upheld in the event of a chemical attack, unless a most explicit caveat were entered on that score. Never mind that NATO is understood to be at an exceptionally severe disadvantage in this aspect of the military balance of terror, as has well been stressed in 'Aspects of Deterrence'. Nor that chemical weapons can proffer alarmingly high dividends to somebody electing to launch a surprise attack, against a background of favourable weather.

Evidently, too, NATO staffs would have to live with 'no first use' whatever course the hostilities took or however long they went on. So would they, if, having continued awhile then died down, full-scale fighting was suddenly resumed. Yet even allowing for what may be some big discrepancies between appearance and reality, the Warsaw Pact seems always to have more scope for the sustained replacement of men and materials, from within earmarked reserves and existing stockpiles, than does NATO. It would almost certainly find it easier as well to embark on crash programmes of production and training. And even if the present differences in these respects were not as pronounced in every aspect as is sometimes assumed, who is to say that they would not become so with the passage of time?

For instance, although the trend towards lower birth-rates has by no means been confined to one side of what we used to call the 'Iron Curtain', it could well affect more critically the manpower situation within NATO. In all probability, too, 'no first use' would have to be adhered to through many other social and cultural changes. Some of these might be far from conducive to martial discipline; heroic sacrifice; alliance cohesion; and all the other attitudes and attributes that could be especially germane to non-nuclear deterrence or defence. Yet those who profess most enthusiasm for such changes include many, on the Left, who now declaim that we must never use nuclear weapons first. Presumably, too, the doctrine could continue to be upheld (see Chapters 2 and 6) regardless of whatever awkward or adverse changes might occur in the geopolitical scene. Among them might be a large-scale military disengagement by the USA from Europe; the emergence of a Soviet leadership more ugly, as suggested below, than what we have at the moment; and a restoration of the Moscow-Peking axis. At the same time, however, it ought to allow for the possibility of mutual thinning out or other local agreements on arms control.

Here two particular contradictions present themselves. One is that a prior commitment to 'no first use' would be tantamount to casting away in advance a bargaining chip that just conceivably might secure an agreement on regional disarmanent sufficiently far-reaching to make the above considerations entirely academic. The other is that, unless it were the product of more analytical sophistication than has been customary in this sphere, an agreement on Mutual and Balanced Force Reductions (MBFRs) between two broadly comparable alliances would be liable to leave the military situation less stable than before. This is because a collateral thinning out would increase the scope for rapid territorial gains through offensive action. Obversely, the more thickly troops were spread on the ground, the easier it ought to be to sustain a defensive campaign. Here a good analogy to draw is with scratch football, played on a standard pitch. If there are five boys on each side, the goals come frequently. If there are 25, goals never come at all. The inference to be drawn is that it would be most unwise ever to sign an MBFR accord unless this could be underwritten by the nuclear sanction.

Surely, too, it is almost inconceivable that NATO could assume a 'no first use' stance in, to take the main focus of interest, West Germany, without each and every Western country incurring similar obligations throughout the world. West Berlin and NATO Scandinavia would always have to be covered thus. So would South-Eastern Europe. So would the North Atlantic and all the other High Seas. So would the Persian Gulf, Korea, the Falkland Islands and wherever else one cares to mention. All the places just cited (the Falklands not excluded) could prove even more susceptible to non-nuclear attack than might the Federal Republic. Yet a major defeat in any of them could have disastrous consequences, either directly or through 'knock-on' effects. Nor would such fateful logic be at all helpful to the aim of halting the proliferation of nuclear weapons to countries that do not currently possess them. Granted, received wisdom on the Left has it that NATO's continuing reliance on nuclear weapons positively encourages such a spread; and that the retention of independent deterrents by Britain and France further accentuates this tendency. However, there is little reason to believe that modern nation states are humble enough merely to follow whatever precedents are set by certain of their peers in different situations. In any case, several countries that might contemplate organising their own nuclear deterrents might actually prefer to justify them on a 'no first use' basis. Irrespective of whether that applied in particular cases, however, all the indications are that such extra-European states as Japan, South Korea, Taiwan, India, Pakistan, Israel, Egypt and South Africa might be far more disposed to 'go nuclear' if they felt that their security was not being properly underwritten by Western assurances and capabilities. Much the same also applies to such European states as Sweden, Yugoslavia and Turkey.

Besides, suppose a country like Israel or Pakistan (to take two plausible examples) felt unable to commit itself never to use its nuclear weapons to avert a non-nuclear defeat. Does one cut off, once and for all, every bit of military or nuclear assistance? If not, one would blatantly lack the courage of one's convictions. Nor do the objections to 'no first use' stem merely from the imperatives of deterring wars or prosecuting them. Relevant, too, is the issue of how they might be terminated, bearing in mind that an outright military victory would very generally be precluded, for the West and its friends, by the balance of military advantage, local and also global. For suppose there was a leadership in the Kremlin that, being fascisto-Marxist in outlook, had been sufficiently ruthless or (see below) desperate to launch an aggressive war in central Europe. Let us assume, too, that this aggression was being held in check. Might not a regime of the character thus indicated come then to see great political attractions in the indefinite prolongation of sporadic and low-intensity conflict in the said theatre and perhaps elsewhere? To be more explicit, might it not feel that such a state of affairs could well help it to keep Communist societies suitably closed, yet exacerbate the divisive strains endemic within the open societies of the West? This, after all, was how the Korean war rumbled on for two years until (in the early aftermath of Stalin's death) the deadlock in the negotiation at Panmunjon was broken by covert but quite explicit American threats of nuclear escalation. David Rees well recognised this 20 years ago[2], and the point has been confirmed since.

Indeed, the continuation of this campaign affords stark confirmation of the proposition that the liberal values we seek to preserve and promote cannot well flourish against such a background. For while it encouraged extreme manifestations of Stalinism throughout the Soviet bloc (China most certainly included), it was also the main impetus behind the McCarthyite 'witch-hunts' in the United States. Among the other ramifications was a pronounced polarisation of politics across Western Europe, the polarity being especially marked over the rearmament of Western Germany. NATO had requested this, contrary to its previous intentions, three months after the *blitzkrieg* invasion of South Korea in June 1950. Nor is a localised land war the only kind of scenario to reckon with. Consider, for example, one in which every merchant ship on the North Atlantic had to sail in convoy on order to shield itself against what might be only sporadic attacks by

Soviet submarines. The likelihood is that the continuation of such a state of affairs, over many weeks or months, would induce a 'garrison-state' syndrome that would jar badly with the ethos of late twentieth-century Western society. At all events, the added logistical and administrative strain would be extremely constrictive and costly.

So regardless of whatever might then be the technical status of Anti-Submarine Warfare (ASW) or the strength of the maritime forces available to each side, NATO would ultimately face just two alternatives. One would be to seek to block the egress to the North Atlantic of any Soviet or other Warsaw Pact submarines: a stratagem which, if successfully sustained, could progressively compromise the Soviet strategic deterrent (see Chapter 3). The other would be to use tactical nuclear weapons to force a ceasefire. It might well be more dissuasive and less dangerous.

Yet the crux of the matter may not be whether the strain of belligerency could be endured for weeks or months. Instead, it may be whether a major economic crisis could be averted, through emergency action by banks and governments, for more than a few days. Among the grounds for apprehension on this score is the degree of financial interdependence that now obtains between the West and the Soviet bloc. By this is meant, above all else, the fact that scores of billions of dollars are owed by the latter to the former. Its significance is that the international monetary system has lately become so bizarre and fragile that creditors may stand uncomfortably exposed to ruthless behaviour by big debtors, not least when these are professing Leninists with *dirigiste* economies and what could be presented as ideological justifications for debt renunciation. After all, even one such act of renunciation might trigger a succession of others around the world. Let us recall, for example, the attitude displayed towards Mexico's debt crisis in 1982 by the six central bankers (among them Signore Lamberto Dini of the Bank of Italy) who guide the strategy of the Bank of International Settlements in Basle: 'the issue for the inner club was not the welfare of that country but as Dini put it, "the stability of the entire banking system" '.[3] Needless to say, a similar reaction played a salient part in shaping the attitude of Western governments towards the more extended political and economic crisis then being faced by Poland. Much the same applied, during the Falklands war, *vis-à-vis* Argentina (see Chapter 6).

Nor would it be adequate for anybody to object that some such talk about a European war being economically unviable was to be heard well before 1914. For one thing, much of the protest then made by Norman Angell and others was not that a war would directly induce a financial collapse but merely that, for each and every party, the cost would far exceed any benefit. For another, the potential linkage between military hostilities and acute financial strain is a lot more menacing today, in several respects, than during the approach of either the First or the Second World War. Thus the period between 1890 and 1914 was *the* era of the 'gold standard': the years in which virtually all currencies were solidly based on this precious metal. By 1939, reliance on gold was receding. However, a general restoration of fixed exchange rates plus the emergence of several informal but highly functional currency blocs had helped to buttress the international monetary system. Today, that system is very much a unity once more, and thus all the more fragile. For while the enormous explosion of information that is taking place in this sphere, as in so many others, may facilitate the handling of small to medium crises, it may actually accelerate and so accentuate the development of more major ones. Meanwhile, gold is ill-placed to act as a universal backer, not least because its residual aura continues to weaken. Problems of acceptability also circumscribe the Special Drawing Rights (SDRs) or 'paper gold' first launched by the International Monetary Fund some 17 years ago and then heralded as set to become, within a decade or so, the medium for most trade between states. At present, SDRs constitute under five per cent of the international liquidity base. Meanwhile, the principle of 'managed float' exchange rates, introduced just over a decade ago, has not led to as much stability between national currencies as was originally hoped. It has not worked smoothly enough.

Above all, however, the world economic order is presently carrying quite a heavy load of international debt, much too high a proportion of which is in the form of short-term loans obtained less for productive investment than to cover trade deficits mainly caused by the rising cost of imported energy. Early in 1983, the total volume of international indebtedness was 700 billion dollars: some 300 of this being owed by Latin America and another 80 by the Soviet bloc. Yet the total amount of currency available worldwide for the financing of foreign trade and related transactions was 400 billion dollars. Granted, these two totals do not have to relate to each other in any exact way. Even so, the size and direction of the difference between them highlights the latent instabilities. No doubt it would still be possible, in principle, to create quite a lot of extra liquidity 'at a stroke' by raising the official price of gold and perhaps then to use this to compensate swiftly banks afflicted by debt renegation. However, such a scheme might be hard to prepare given a background of military hostilities and the mutual suspicion that customarily obtains between political leaders and central bankers. In any case, too ready a recourse to such a measure might be seen in some quarters as too dangerous a precedent. Furthermore, the USSR might stand to gain too much, this by virtue of its still being a major gold producer. Some governments might also feel this, even with such a contingency on their hands, about South Africa.

Besides, the threat may take a more tangible form than rescripts or reneging on debt or other psychological blows to confidence. It could involve the physical destruction of nodal parts of the banking infrastructure. By way of illustration, let us make reference again to the Bank of International Settlements. Looked at as an institution, this is a body which lays claim to 40 billion dollars of securities, not a little of it on loan to Eastern Europe. Looked at as real estate, it is a new building complex in Basle, with many miles of underground storage tunnels but also with 18 stories above the ground and so highly exposed to even non-nuclear air attack. What can be said apropos of Basle broadly applies to Zurich, Frankfurt, London and other financial centres in Europe and elsewhere. From all of which, the conclusion seems ineluctably to emerge that, for fiscal reasons alone, it is simply not worth preparing to avoid the early introduction of nuclear weapons into a

European war. For much delay could all too easily lead to the precipitate collapse of the financial system of the Western world: a prospect that might, of course, be seen by fascisto-Marxist elements in Moscow and other Communist capitals as a positive inducement to bring about or persist with a showdown in Europe.

Next to be considered is the greater dependence of Western Europe on the USA that would be implicit in reduced nuclear reliance, the connection being the added premium that would then be attached to American military manpower and high technology. Of course, it is only fair to say that some advocates of 'no first use' or something approaching it have always remained strong for the Atlantic Alliance, therefore need not feel acute qualms on this score.[4] But others, especially on the far Left, have either always been or have lately become zealously critical of many specific US policies and, indeed, comprehensively scornful of her overall role in the world. Still, to dwell long on such inconsistencies would be to trivialise a desperately important aspect of this whole subject. Our own opinion is as follows. The preservation of the Atlantic Alliance is of the highest importance for Europe, for North America, and for Mankind at large. Not merely does it afford a counterbalance to the Soviet bloc; it also constrains the USA from sliding into the xenophobic illiberalism of its radical Right. But a precondition of the continuation of this trans-oceanic axis on an equitable, stable and constructive basis must surely be Western Europe's dialogue with its North American partners with the authority that comes from knowing that, if the USA and Canada ever did feel impelled to withdraw, it could still make some provision for its own defence. Yet it is hard to imagine how Western Europe could entertain that hope if a new received wisdom required the categoric renunciation of nuclear first use, early or even at all.

Naturally, however, nothing we may say will cut much ice with those who either openly aver or inwardly believe that, never mind what NATO says or does, the probability of Communist aggression against NATO Europe is about as high as, let us say, a Finnish invasion of Uruguay. But to them, several elementary points must be made. The first is that the information explosion that gathers pace around the world will oblige every authoritarian regime, be it Red or Blue or hybrid, to make an ever-starker choice between becoming more open and devolved or else ever more centralised and repressive.

The rub herein for the USSR derives from its being decidedly multi-national in character, with its non-Russian peoples being mainly distributed around its perimeter. For this means that the pressures towards more economic or political or cultural freedom tend to differentiate along national or communal lines, with the minority nationalities taking the more liberal stance on most issues most of the time. Therefore, the choice presented by modernisation against such a background of national pluralism could readily turn into one between greater repression and creeping disintegration. The contradiction in question goes far to explain why the relatively optimistic view of the Soviet future that became so characteristic of the Khruschev years no less visibly waned under Brezhnev. More specifically, there is compelling evidence that the full-scale invasion of Afghanistan in 1979 was eventually decided on chiefly in order to contain restiveness within the central Asian republics of the USSR.[5] Evidently, however, it is still the several nationalities inside the European borders of the USSR which pose potentially the biggest problem on this account. Ironically, too, this problem is compounded by comparable contradictions within the sphere of direct control that Moscow established in Eastern Europe, through Cold War haggling and coercion, between 1944 and 1949. Indeed, her recurrent interference in the internal affairs of the other countries in Eastern Europe has to be read as a latter-day application of the 'domino theory'. Should the spirit of liberalism progress in Poland, say, it might then spread to the Baltic States, the Ukraine and other constituent parts of the Soviet Union itself.

Moreover, a confused concern thus to constrain and distort Communist development is always liable to induce Moscow to wax more belligerent on the global plane. Yet so far as her scope for actual military action is concerned, a sharp dichotomy is readily to be observed. Her North Eurasian geography puts the USSR in a position to exert physical pressure virtually anywhere along a circumferential zone from Finnmark through Iran and Afghanistan to Manchuria. At the same time, however, it constrains her projections of power to more distant places. So what one has here is a geostrategic situation that almost invites the penultimate horror of what can be termed Limited World War. By which is meant a pattern of conflict in which the Soviet Union or maybe the West elects to retaliate forcibly in some other theatre against a localised thrust by the adversary alliance which it refuses to countenance but is unable to cope with in the locality in question.[6] Evidently, nowhere would afford Moscow more scope and incentive for such a riposte than West Berlin and Western Europe would in circumstances in which the deterrent posture of NATO had lost credibility, perhaps through political dissension within the alliance or else because of some disastrous lapse in operational doctrine, such as the adoption of 'no first use'.

If nuclear weapons can have a deterrent value against nuclear attack or blackmail (a proposition that is very widely conceded), it seems to some of us a matter of elementary logic that they can also have such value against 'conventional' or 'chemical' threats. But were deterrence to fail, they might have to be used to secure conflict termination on the basis of a military stand-off coupled with the cessation of any blatantly aggressive acts of economic warfare. Nevertheless, it would be quite wrong for the West ever to depart from the principle that nuclear release would always have to be authorised by the political heads of state of those countries most closely involved. For one thing, the precept of civil control over the military is fundamental to Western liberal democracy. For another, it is impossible to draw up in advance contingency plans able to anticipate at all precisely the complex development of a warlike crisis or how moods may change the while. Therefore, political control could not generally be effective without active political involvement in the particularities of crisis management.

As regards the all-important inter-German sector, the due exercises of this prerogative would normally mean the deferment for several days of the initial nuclear release. For only this would allow enough time for the following

preliminaries to be properly accomplished: the compilation of a
full data base on the military situation; a synoptic appreciation
thereof; extensive discussions among the governments
concerned of the policy options; negotiations with the USSR
and its allies about the conflict in Europe and also
confrontations anywhere else (like the Middle East) that may
bear directly on it; making what provision can be made against
social and financial stress; and the actual authorisation of
nuclear delivery.

Yet it is hard to see what would ever be gained from further
delay in response. Acute social and political strains might
appear in Western countries, thanks not least to televisual
'direct action' by elements within what arrogates to itself the
title of 'peace movement'. Indeed, certain insurgent groups
might seize this unique opportunity to do their very worst.
Meanwhile, the shock that war would perforce administer to
the world financial system would assuredly be compounded
(perhaps to an irremediable extent) by a prolongation thus of
hostilities. Meanwhile, the military situation would become
ever harder to understand and interpret. In all probability, too,
it would become more menacing in terms either of attrition and
exhaustion or else of the front being broken or the Rhine being
reached. After all, this mighty river lies a mere 90 miles from
the inter-German border, down the Fulda gap. Yet once
Warsaw Pact troops were standing on its eastern bank, they
would enjoy a decisive advantage in lateral manoeuvre. Worse
still, their governments would be left in a devastatingly strong
bargaining position in the event of a cease-fire and
negotiations. Besides, even if the front was holding and the
relative erosion of military strength not too unfavourable, this
would probably be partly because NATO had been trading a
certain amount of space for time. Yet it has surprisingly little
scope for doing this at all, without leaving in Communist hands
some important districts within West Germany. Thus towns
and cities within 30 miles of the inter-German border include
(from north to south) Lübeck, Hamburg, Braunschweig,
Göttingen, Kassel, Schweinfurt, Coburg and Bayreuth. Nor
should we forget that just a few days procrastination could
strongly encourage an extension into Limited World War.

Moreover, it is only too easy to imagine circumstances in which nuclear release should and could be authorised within a considerably shorter time span, the urgency being the greater and the issues more clear cut. Naked nuclear aggression would certainly be one case in point. Chemical attack might well be another. So might any surprise attack, launched massively and in great depth. So might one focused on the infrastructure of command and control or the reinforcement stockpiles. So might concurrent attacks in, say, Europe and the Middle East or Korea: a form of Limited World War. So might a mining of the approaches to key Western ports. So, indeed, might a deliberate attempt to engineer, by non-violent means, a Western financial crash. Not that anybody in their right mind is going to suggest that the release of nuclear weapons is devoid of risk. To start with, nobody denies that it would always constitute a considerable and very visible act of escalation. Yet not infrequently in the history of war, one party or the other has misjudged the consequences of deliberate escalation of hostilities, whether this be in regard to (a) increasing the depth or width of the battle zone, (b) introducing new weapons or (c) attacking new kinds of target. Thus there has often been a disposition to overestimate the intimidatory effect on the enemy and to discount the extent to which it angers and embitters him.

Therefore, it is obvious that indefinite reliance on the crude mechanics and even cruder psychology of the balance of terror is less agreeable and secure than would be a genuine and profound *détente* underwritten by equitable and verifiable agreements on arms control and phased disarmament. But in the absence of so benign a regimen, it is entirely legitimate to ask whether a strategy that involves early nuclear release might not involve less risk to the West and, indeed, to world civilisation than would the immediate alternatives.

CHAPTER TWO

THE CONTROL OF ESCALATION

Straight away this much has to be conceded. If there is anything about which the bulk of lay opinion throughout the West is at least vaguely in agreement with the 'peace movement', it is its contention that release of one nuclear weapon anywhere is bound rapidly to lead to the release of virtually all of them everywhere, certainly if the confrontation in question is between the two main alliances. This is seen as inescapable corollary of the unique awfulness of these devices.

Yet whether it enjoys a goodly measure of overt and tacit popular endorsement or whether it does not, the inference thus being drawn is spurious. It probably owes too much to the survival, within a collective subconscious, of the notion fashionable some thirty years ago (though invalid even then) that a 'nuclear explosion' necessarily meant, in operational terms, the detonation of a 'hydrogen bomb' above a large city. It evidently owes too much to the lurid sense of apocalyptic doom that is part and parcel of the millenarianism which suffuses the contemporary 'peace movement' and likewise led some of its progenitors (like Bertrand Russell and C.P. Snow) to make predictions about the imminence of nuclear catastrophe that have already been discredited by the passage of time. It owes nothing to logic nor, for that matter, to common sense. Thus other things being equal, one might expect a first localised use of such devices to reveal their dreadfulness so starkly as to cause all sides to recoil in horror from their further employment and hence from continued warfare of any kind.

Either way, however, it would not be fruitful to pursue the question further on so abstract a plane. What has to be considered is what operational philosophy, force posture and ambient circumstances may allow the prospects for the control of escalation to be kept within tolerable bounds. What ought also to be considered more frequently is whether a non-nuclear war might not be prone to extend far more readily than an incipient nuclear exchange. Also whether this tendency might not be strongly reinforced by a prior commitment on the part of the West not to release nuclear weapons under any circumstances. So what has become imperative, for this reason but also for others, is a shift of emphasis within the nuclear debate from pure ethics to constructive pragmatism. Included in the latter must be a revaluation of the relevant parts of operational doctrine.

If one looks back some twenty years, one can observe such a progression. With the first upsurge of the Campaign for Nuclear Disarmanent (CND), during the years after the explosion of a British hydrogen device in 1957, the argument had focused tightly, especially within Britain itself, on what were presented as stark moral choices. By the early sixties, however, more and more discussion was taking place, throughout the West, about how actually to manage a warlike confrontation between NATO and the Warsaw Pact. Still, the contribution made by British thinkers to this debate, during the several years it was dominant, was circumscribed by a number of factors. So in effect, just two schools of nuclear theory emerged, the one centred on Washington and the other on Paris. Needless to say, their differences related to the respective locations and military-cum-industrial strengths of the USA and France. As indicated below, however, they stemmed as well from more deep-rooted cultural differences. The dialectic thus generated remains utterly basic to the overriding problem of the control of escalation. Therefore, we ought now to examine it further, this in conjunction with some consideration of its interplay with Soviet thought.[1]

During the Kennedy era (1960-63), the American body of doctrine came to be known as 'flexible response'; this term usually being employed in a broader or perhaps looser sense than it was soon to be within NATO. In essence, the argument ran thus: 'It would be foolish to threaten all-out nuclear war in response to a local challenge made by an adversary – e.g. the USSR as she will be by 1970 – possessed of an ultimate capacity for overwhelming retaliation in every conceivable circumstance. So what is required is an ability to keep all crises firmly under central political and military direction, this in order to modulate all counter-moves in the light of enemy actions and the progress or otherwise of diplomatic bargaining.' Measures contingently taken might involve resort to nothing other than 'conventional' or perhaps tactical nuclear weapons. In some situations, on the other hand, there could be an actual or threatened initiation of what came to be known as 'Limited Strategic War', the slow-motion or selective release of strategic weapons in order to achieve certain material and psychological ends. Among the more recent encapsulations of this notion has been the Presidential Directive 59 signed by President Carter in July 1980. For this called for (a) more plans for less than all-out strikes against the USSR, (b) the inclusion within these of the targetting of administrative 'nodes' in such a way as to threaten the continued functioning of the Soviet political system, (c) and added emphasis on the survivability not just of US strategic forces but of their command and control facilities, and (d) an improvement in 'look-shoot-look' capability, with special reference to the assessment of nuclear strikes against Soviet targets.

However, advocates of flexible response in whatever form have always insisted that no country could ever sustain such a strategy against the homeland of a major opponent unless its own strategic forces were sophisticated, large and varied. For one thing, it would have to remain ready and able to deliver suitably severe riposte in the event of some further massive act of escalation on the part of the adversary. For another, a more subtle modulation of the use of strategic weapons would depend on a substantial quantity being available to start with.

Herein lay the rationale for the doubts entertained by some leading members of the Kennedy administration about the relevance, in the Atlantic Alliance context, of the relatively small independent deterrents being built up by Britain and

France respectively. These doubts were made bluntly explicit by Secretary of Defense McNamara in the keynote speech he delivered on the Ann Arbor campus of the University of Michigan in June 1962. For he then contended that 'limited nuclear capabilities, operating independently are dangerous, expensive, prone to obsolescence, and lacking in credibility as a deterrent'. Never mind that Washington was already actively engaged in helping to modernise the British force by means of Skybolt or, as events soon transpired, Polaris. It has always been only too easy to understand that, to analysts entirely sold on flexible strategic response, the British and French forces cannot look other than inadequate, not to say otiose. All else apart, those two nations have lacked enough strategic nuclear warheads to employ them much, if at all, on a piecemeal and selective basis. Nor, indeed, does either show much sign of being able to wage non-nuclear war against continental heartlands by means of extended-range cruise-missiles armed with high-explosive or chemical payloads: a capability already being actively canvassed by some circles in the USA and, in all probability, the USSR. Besides, submarines would not be very suitable as delivery platforms in the rather complicated context of limited or slow-motion strategic war. The old argument about sea-mobile systems being relatively inaccurate probably counts for little or nothing these days. But difficulties over communication might develop and could matter more during a slow-motion exchange of this sort than in respect of a single full-scale retaliatory strike. Nor should one entirely disregarded the truism that the release from under the water of one ballistic missile is liable *ipso facto* to betray the current position of the remainder on board: 15 in the case of the existing French and British boats. Granted, none of these objections could apply with quite as much force to the French deterrent because this does include even now a land-based missile component of considerable size. Nor, indeed, would they be relevant to its British counterpart unless a national option of graduated strategic action was of real interest to the government of the day in London. So far that premise has never applied.

Not that diversity or quality or numerical strength can in themselves resolve all the difficulties that might surround the application by the United States of the precept of Limited Strategic War. Among the more fundamental of them relates to the underlying assumption that the Russians think along much the same lines. For it is not entirely certain whether they do or ever would. Thus one influence at work in the Kremlin is a continental European tradition whereby warfare is seen as inherently too incoherent either for close analysis or for tight control. Whereas Anglo-American military insights have mainly stemmed from a long succession of operations around or across very distant shores, the Russians (and, no less, the Germans and the French) recall much experience of mass mobilisation followed by savage and chaotic general war, this all too often extending deep into their own homelands. As it happens, it was a distinctly Eurocentric English bard who conjured the metaphor of ignorant armies clashing by night. No matter, the image of war encapsulated by this phrase is akin to the Prussian perception as epitomised by Karl von Clausewitz. For if there is one message which comes across, above all others, in the studied convolutions of this pioneer of strategic thought, it is that military violence is inherently too rough and clumsy to lend itself at all well to exact modulation.

His representative character is well confirmed by the evident bearing his work has had on the formulation of Soviet perspectives on war. He himself rose up from the same Hegelian ambience as did Marx. Furthermore, Lenin made detailed notes on his writings, notes to which he occasionally alluded. Meanwhile, Leo Tolstoy, a titanic literary influence and a contemporary of Clausewitz, dismissed no less readily the very idea of assured control. He even managed to persuade himself that it was invalid in that it was a corollary of what he saw as the erroneous philosophy of freewill, a confusion that is manifested time and again in the pages of *War and Peace*. Predictably enough, the public Russian reaction to the burgeoning American interest in various patterns of flexible response was to dismiss it as not only naively unreal but thoroughly unethical. Granted, the Soviets did themselves come to accept during the sixties that there could be a significant (perhaps an indefinite?) phase of non-nuclear war, as witness the large-scale non-nuclear manoeuvres (Exercise

Dnepr) held in the Ukraine in 1967. Still, neither their published doctrine nor their observed training has ever yet lent encouragement to the view that a war might continue to be limited once it had gone nuclear.

Duly, the 1982 working-party report to the Church of England Synod, *The Church and the Bomb*, concluded that the Soviet leadership refuses to 'believe in flexible response' (p.145): the implication being that they themselves would, on being attacked, 'almost certainly retaliate with all the forces at their disposal' (p.45)[2]. In other words, the 'idea that nuclear war can be kept limited' has to be dismissed as 'implausible' (p.18). Indeed, we are even advised that 'No one denies' that the prospects for checking nuclear escalation short of 'all-out war' are 'poor' (pp.29-30). In fact, of course, there are very many analysts in the West who would readily disavow so categoric a judgment. Nor may they be without covert support from their counterparts on the Soviet side. After all, the Kremlin has openly threatened, on three distinct occasions, to launch long-range rockets, on a selective basis, in response to a specific challenge. Each time the evident reason was its continuing inability to project balanced theatre forces much beyond the Eurasian confines of the USSR. Each time, too, it would have been impracticable to fire enough rockets to be militarily effective, save that they were fitted with nuclear or strong chemical warheads. The most famous instance was the strident, though blatantly disingenuous, warning about rocket strikes against London and Paris made by Marshal Bulganin as the Suez campaign was drawing to its close in 1956. Then in 1960 the Soviet leadership was to throw down two more challenges of similar form and perhaps more substance. During the crisis that May over U-2 reconnaissance flights across Soviet territory, Marshal Malinovsky warned of instant retaliation against whatever bases any further flights were dispatched from. Similarly, in July, Mr Khruschev himself was to speak of rocket reprisals in the event of an American attack on Cuba.

All of which does cast in a curious light the USSR's doctrinal dismissals of the possibility of graduating a nuclear conflict. But so, too, do other aspects of the record. As is well known, a recurrent strand in Soviet maritime doctrine has been a putative requirement to engage hostile Fleet Ballistic Missile (FBM) submarines or maybe large fleet carriers, as they approach within striking distance of the Soviet Union. Yet this cannot make the slightest practical or even logical sense, unless it be held to betoken a concept of partial or slow-motion strategic war. Similarly, no attempt to relate Soviet declaratory doctrine to the observed size and configuration of Warsaw Treaty armies as well as to parallel doctrinal statements about other aspects of modern land war (logistics; fire and movement etc), can be successful without an interpretation less naive than *The Church and the Bomb* allows. What this need be is that, while Moscow and its allies assuredly remain utterly scornful of certain American-inspired notions about the very subtle and exact modulation of deterrence, they do see nuclear firepower as separable into several distinct steps. Not all of these may be brought actively into play during a particular conflict. But even those retained in limbo may have an overhanging influence.

During the sixties, a French nuclear version of the continentalist perspective on war forcefully emerged. Its point of departure was that, of its very nature, a nuclear war would be an all-or-nothing (*tout en rien*) encounter. Therefore, a diversity of notional response options is not what matters. Instead, it is the exercise of sovereign authority over the deterrent force in question. Likewise, the Gaullists, in particular, stressed that such sovereignty was inherently national and hence indivisible. Hence it was, in their view, futile if not individious to talk of multinational participation in the formulation of nuclear policy, either before a crisis or during one. As Foreign Minister Michel Debré was to remark in 1970, there will always be 'the integrated who follow, and integrator who commands'. A related precept was that 'the substitution of the balance of power ... for the United States monopoly in this field has transformed the general conditions of Western defence'.[3] That is to say, the advent of nuclear parity between the Superpowers is bound to make Washington much more reluctant to authorise nuclear release in defence of Europe, lest she thereby bring a *tout ou rien* onslaught down on herself and other American cities. Conversely, the French deterrent would act as a shield for neighbouring countries because it would automatically come into full play as nuclear strikes upon any one of them spread uncontrollably over the French border. That element in the thesis had, in fact, been neatly encapsulated by Georges Pompidou in 1964 when, as French Prime Minister, he claimed that the defence of Europe is 'physically and geographically inseparable from that of France, which is not the case with forces outside the European continent, even if allied'.

However, the French authorities themselves were soon to drop their insistence that this neo-Cartesian logic embraced the whole truth. For the retirement of President de Gaulle himself in April 1969 and the death (in an air crash over the Indian Ocean the previous year) of General Ailleret, his Chief of Staff of the armed forces, had left the way open for a reappraisal. Indeed, in an address delivered at the *Institut des Hautes Etudes de Défense Nationale* in the spring of 1969, General Fourquet, the new Chief of Staff, referred to the way 'graduated actions' by tactical nuclear forces might precede a 'strategic strike'. What is more, whereas General Ailleret had described the strategic deterrent as usable in 'all directions' (*tous azimuts*), Fourquet spoke of 'the enemy to the East', against which France's army divisions could expect to fight in 'close co-operation' with her allies. In June 1976, President Giscard d'Estaing addressed the *Institute des Hautes Etudes de Défense Nationale*. He apprehended that *tout ou rien* would lack credibility in the event of 'very major disturbances in neighbouring countries, or uncertainty as to the reaction of one country to a change in the political situation of another'. He saw tactical nuclear systems as potentially 'weapons for battle', not merely as signals of a greater intent. He also laid emphasis on the Presidential control of all nuclear weapons, an emphasis that *ipso facto* negates the proposition that a nuclear response has to take the form of a full-scale reflex action. Evidently, too, the development by France of quite a diversified tactical nuclear echelon is in line with this trend of argument. So, of course, is the interest Paris has lately evinced in the development of a neutron bomb.

Nevertheless, Paris does remain considerably committed to

something not so very far removed from *tout ou rien*, as witness recent remarks by President Mitterand about the essential need for national control and about the deterrent forces of the Superpowers being needlessly large. So the most that ought to be said is that, impelled by their own technical advances, the French have moved closer to the compromise position long held by Britain apropos of the graduation of nuclear responses within a theatre war. Apparently, too, the French share the British sense that a tactical nuclear capability may have a kind of background relevance to operations 'out-of-area'.

In some measure, these oblique compliments are returned. Take, for example, the statement the then Minister of Defence, Francis Pym, made to the House of Commons on 24 January 1980: 'For many years, NATO has had the capability to threaten deep nuclear strikes, reaching as far as the Soviet heartland, with systems based in Europe and separate from the main strategic armoury ... The nuclear decision would be no less agonizing for the UK than for the US. But it would be a decision of a separate and independent power, and a power whose survival in freedom might be more directly threatened by aggression in Europe than that of the US'. What all of this suggests, of course, is that the 'continentalist' and American perspectives need to be blended if NATO is to preserve adequate deterrence against the outbreak of hostilities or, if such an eruption does occur, against the resultant fighting continuing for an unacceptable length of time or taking some unacceptable course. For the fact of the matter is that the European and American nuclear forces stand in a paradoxical relationship to one another, so far as the protection of Western Europe is concerned. The small but indiguenous British and French deterrents would appear at their most credible if a saturation Soviet attack were in the offing, this because they could be expected to come automatically into play in reflex retaliation against the wholesale destruction of their home region. Contrariwise, the American nuclear umbrella (being not only much bigger but also more diversified and sophisticated) would look at its most convincing in the face of threats that were more tightly controlled and pitched at a lower level.

Since neither pattern of conflict can be ruled out, both modes of deterrence are needed. The essential point was succinctly put in 1965 by General André Beaufre, the man who *inter alia* had commanded the French forces at Suez, 'Different methods must simultaneously be used to keep the enemy's mind in that state of uncertainty which alone can render deterrence effective ... to enable several methods of deterrence to be used simultaneously, there must be several *centres of decision*' (his italics).[5] Not that the mere preservation of this complementality affords of itself a sufficient guarantee that deterrence can be preserved or, failing that, conflict escalation duly controlled. The political relationships within the Atlantic Alliance will always be of fundamental importance. By the same token, the dialogue between the West and the Soviet bloc will always have a significant part to play. Moreover, one element in this dialogue will perforce be Communist perception of the likelihood of Western deterrent resolve being vitiated by a polarisation of public opinion within the various countries, be these about Defence or other basic issues (see Chapter 6). Nor is this all. Both the European and American forces in question must be so structured as to ensure their being able to ride out any sudden and full-scale attack sufficiently well to be still able to retaliate overwhelmingly (see Chapter 3). It is similarly important (especially on the American side) that the command-and-control arrangements be adequately survivable. Yet another prerequisite may be operational philosophies that properly relate to the respective force postures and to arms limitation. In which connection, it is of interest to note that the SALT-1 agreement signed by the USA and the USSR in 1972 in effect acknowledged a certain mutality of interest by regarding neither Washington nor Moscow as open to attack. It did so through the incorporation of an Anti-Ballistic Missile (ABM) Treaty that provided *inter alia* for the ABM protection of each 'national command authority'.

Yet if these several conditions can be met, the prospects for the tolerably close control of nuclear confrontation should be adequate for credible deterrence and assured crisis management . Above all, they should be a lot better than those for curbing the spread of non-nuclear hostilities, in circumstances in which the West or some large part thereof had made a solemn commitment never to be first to resort to nuclear weapons. For such a commitment could well be read in Moscow as an open invitation to extend the conflict into a number of different theatres, thereby transmuting it into a Limited World War. To which one has to add that too great and too visible a reluctance, on the part of NATO as such or else of certain Western nations, to authorise nuclear release could have much the same effect. That is to say, an overt commitment to a 'higher nuclear threshold' in central Europe might weaken deterrence, not only there but globally. Suppose for instance, a war involving the Superpowers broke out around the Persian Gulf. The Kremlin might feel inhibited about seeking a clear-cut local victory, fearing the destruction of oilfields on which it might be coming to depend itself. Therefore, it might prefer the escalation of conflict out-of-theatre to its intensification in-theatre. It might, in any case, believe – in broad accordance with the Hegelian dialectic – that a time of decision had come in the global clash of ideologies. Before we knew where we were, fighting might be in progress in Finnmark, central Europe, Yugoslavia, the Gulf still, Korea and the High Seas. There might also be action against military satellites in near Space orbit. In other words, we would have slid into an alarmingly advanced state of Limited World War.

Macabre through such a scenario may seem, it is less far removed from some of our recent experience than may be thought. Almost certainly, for instance, there was a causal link between the way the war in Vietnam was approaching a climax and the intensified skirmishing along the 1953 armistice line in Korea, in 1967 and again in 1968. Nor is it by any means inconceivable that a wish to divert American attention from Vietnam lay behind the curious machinations by the USSR apropos of the Arab-Israel conflict in May 1967, though this is not to say that it had sought the all-out war which was to result from its propagating in Cairo and Damascus the fiction that Israel was preparing for a big attack on Syria. Nor has the USSR seemed unaware of the hostage value of the Western European appendage of Eurasia. Thus during the Cuban crisis of 1962, Khruschev alluded to a possible Soviet invasion of Turkey, then as again today a staunch member of the Atlantic

Alliance. Meanwhile, plans were laid in several capitals lest coercive action was taken against West Berlin. Likewise, the physical albeit non-lethal pressures applied to West Berlin during the early months of 1965 and also of 1968 were respectively coincident with sharp escalations of the Vietnam conflict, no matter that the given reasons were couched strictly in terms of the local situation.

So it is entirely fair to surmise that such interplay could occur again, maybe in a grimmer fashion. Nor should we forget that a commitment to 'no first use' or, at any rate, a 'high threshold' of first use might remove otherwise powerful inhibitions against the escalation of conflict within a theatre. Most crucially, it might remove those against a sudden initiation of conflict by means of a blanket attack by aircraft and missiles. Looking at that particular possibility with reference to central Europe, one is bound to say that one vital facility that could then be particularly at risk is the command-and-control network. Another very important and susceptible one is that comprised of the pre-positioned stockpiles of equipment and basic stores intended to accoutre two (being expanded to four) US army divisions plus some air support, which have been earmarked for despatch across the North Atlantic air bridge in the event of an emergency. Considered as potential targets, these stockpiles and their infrastructure are inherently static, large, visible and soft. What is more, it would not be too difficult for the Warsaw Pact to concoct some sort of political excuse for launching a 'surgical strike' against them, ahead of other hostilities.

Next, there is the problem of de-escalation. For various reasons, this may be easier to handle in the case of nuclear weapons. The extra fear they engender may transcend considerations of relative tactical advantage. Besides, much thought has already been addressed to their top-level political and military control. Moreover, one concrete result of all this cerebration (within the Warsaw Pact as well as within NATO and the other Western command structures) has been specific arrangements designed to ensure that the authorisation of release is kept under tight central control. Over and beyond all of which, the unique and discrete nature of nuclear warheads is conducive to their control being centralised yet specific. So much for *tout ou rien*, depicted as an eternal verity. Once a non-nuclear Limited World War had really got going, however, it might be virtually impossible to set into reverse. Too many nations might become involved. So might too many insurgent and protest movements. Most of these parties would have local aims to pursue or scores to settle. Some of them might find their own military hard to restrain. Meanwhile, the world's financial markets would be experiencing one disintegrative shock after another. Indeed, it is all too easy to imagine a Limited World War sliding into such a state of chaos that chemical and nuclear weapons started to be used in far less restrained and discriminating a fashion than might have been the case if doctrine had allowed for their relatively early application to the original sector of conflict. In short, it is impossible to avoid the conclusion that concern about the management of escalation and de-escalation affords another compelling argument against 'no first use' or 'no early use'. In other words, the prevailing notions about this aspect of the problem are almost diametrically wrong.

Nor is this conclusion to be gainsayed by suggestions that everything has been said above is far too logical, that it does not take enough account of the 'irrationality' factor in human affairs. Certainly, attitudes that are irrational on almost any definition often play their part in initiating or sustaining aggression. But one does not have to be much of a cynic to perceive that the instigators thereof have a marked capacity to become much more rational and circumspect when their own homelands arc liable to be savaged and when they themselves, plus their friends and relations, are liable to be killed. It is a brutal yet simple truth which can be illustrated well enough by the behaviour of the leading fascist dictatorships of the Second World War. If in 1941 Imperial Japan had been possessed of a due capacity for dispassionate reflection, she would have accepted that it was far better to accede to Western demands to withdraw from China than to commence hostilities against Britain, Holland and the USA. But that December, she adopted the latter course of action, despite extreme apprehension within her own ruling circles as to where it would lead her. Already the gravest doubts were entertained about her own ability to withstand a strategic counter-offensive within the Pacific. Yet at the same time, there was little desire to see an outright global victory by Nazi Germany, ostensibly her vital ally. So all that the authorities in Tokyo could hope for was that their country would be left as the arbiter of a German-American stalemate, a balance almost certainly too delicate to achieve and patently too delicate to last. Then in 1944 a strategic air offensive began against the imperial homeland itself, an offensive that was to reach its climax with the dropping of two nuclear bombs in August 1945. Evidently, the fascist leadership could have resolved to fight on a while, perhaps using prisoners-of-war and occupied peoples as hostages. This time, however, it decided with some alacrity to 'endure the unendurable' and surrender. Never mind that this capitulation had to be far more of a total one than what had been called for in 1941.

Likewise, Nazi Germany was in desperate straits by the end of 1944. On the other hand, she did have substantial stocks of shells and bombs loaded (or loadable) with nerve gas. Also, she was suffused by a Wagnerian sense of *götterdammerung*. Furthermore, she was also proving only too ready to use poison gas without pity or remorse on millions of Jews, gypsies and other helpless deportees. Nevertheless, she used neither nerve gas or any other toxic chemicals against the Allied troops invading her nor against their homelands. An Anglo-American ability to retaliate in kind is generally held to be a crucial factor in this restraint. So, too, in this nuclear era, a manifest capacity on the part of its adversaries for massive strategic retaliation cannot but act as a powerful inhibition against any party escalating a nuclear exchange out of all proportion. By so doing, it presents the possibility that nuclear firepower may be applied to the minimal extent necessary to enforce a military stand-off within the original theatre of conflict.

How then does this precept relate to the present course of the arms race as between the major nations? Are the prospects for the use of nuclear weapons as a means of conflict curtailment enhanced by the state of the nuclear arms balance? Is the case for preparing to employ them in this way being affected by manifold changes in regard to other kinds of warfare?

CHAPTER THREE

THE CHANGING FACE OF WAR

Perhaps the most pertinent point of departure is the following. However unstable the world situation may appear overall, there is a salient military respect in which, in the judgment of not a few of us, has lately evolved from dynamic instability to stable equilibrium. Thus since the late sixties, each of the Superpowers has possessed the ability to inflict utterly unendurable damage on its chief rival by way of retaliation or under all other circumstances. What is more, neither can seriously hope ever to change this situation to its advantage, whether by a breakthrough in relevant areas of weapons technology or through a surge in the production of existing systems. Qualitative or quantitative change can and will alter progressively the said equilibirium's appearance. What it cannot now do is overturn it. Mutual Assured Destruction (MAD) is a veritable revolution in military affairs, one with profound implications for any recourse to nuclear firepower.

What strategic analysts would these days virtually all agree on, is this. The biggest and most durable impediment to a disabling strategic strike at this level is that presented by the mobility at sea, coupled with high immunity from detection, of the many Fleet Ballistic Missile (FBM) submarines possessed by each Superpower plus the ten operated by Britain and France. Nor can this conclusion be invalidated simply by allusions to the ultimate ascendancy of Anti-Submarine Warfare (ASW) in such previous campaigns as the Battle of the Atlantic (1939-45). An FBM flotilla is never concerned, as were the U-Boats of World War Two, with closing to action with enemy vessels. Instead, its duty is to avoid them, an aim which is much assisted by the special attributes its boats derive from nuclear propulsion and from the novel hull designs associated with it. Obversely, the progress in submarine detection achieved since 1945 has been decidedly modest, certainly in relation to the huge investments made in the relevant areas of research and development. Nor are the underlying reasons hard to fathom. They relate considerably to the geometry of wave motion (see below), interpreted in relation to the dimensions of the High Seas. They derive as well from the waters themselves being almost opaque to electromagnetic emission at almost any frequency; and from their also being very prone to absorb, mask, refract or reflect sound waves.

Besides, it is not just a matter of whether ASW could be directed against an FBM flotilla as forcefully as it was against the U-Boats. A far more exacting criterion has to be applied. For even in May 1943 – a month of decisive victory for the Allied escort forces on North Atlantic stations – the average attrition of the U-Boat fleet at sea was barely 1.0 per cent per day. Yet a pre-emptive first-strike against an FBM flotilla would have to achieve close to 100 per cent in under a quarter of an hour: a needful advance in performance of the order of 10,000, expressed in those terms.[1] True, the FBM balance is not quite equal as yet. The Soviet fleet continues to lack the reliability and endurance needed to negate completely the geographical constraints on its deployment. However, this is a circumstance that will be transformed as more of the new Typhoon-class vessels enter service. Meanwhile, whatever operational disadvantages the USSR still labours under in this sphere are offset by her numerical preponderance, in respect not only of Submarine-Launched Ballistic Missiles (SLBMs) but also of the Intercontinental Ballistic Missiles (ICBMs) deployed on land. Also by the fact that Moscow like Washington has installed altogether about ten times as many strategic nuclear warheads as would be required to reduce the urban-based civilisation of the adversary alliance to a state of hapless desolation. So the dust-clouds from a 'counterforce' pre-emptive strike, one heavy enough to reduce even the respective ICBM forces below a level sufficient to carry out so macabre a retaliation, would most probably produce a ferocious 'nuclear winter' all across the Northern Hemisphere. Surface temperatures would drop several tens of degrees Celsius within a few weeks and stay low for months.[2]

Nor is the deadlock here indicated likely to be broken (as opposed to complicated) by an eventual introduction of Space-based battle-stations, mounting beam weapons intended to protect friendly territories against incoming strategic rockets. For there are cogent grounds for doubting whether this form of Ballistic Missile Defence (BMD), now the subject of exotic exploratory research in the USA at least, could ever improve at all decisively the survival prospects, in the face of surprise attack, of the capacities of the USA (or, for that matter, the USSR) for nuclear destruction. Could such a screen ever shield adequately society at large? Above all, could it conceivable cost a Superpower less to create and maintain than its chief adversary would have to expend to swamp or otherwise thwart it?

To start with, nobody would deny that there are three ineluctable drawbacks to placing weapons beyond the confines of the Earth and its atmosphere. No blast affect can be registered in a near vacuum. External control becomes more difficult. Extra costs are incurred. But nobody denies either that there are two big attractions. From, say, 100 miles up the horizon is nearly 1,000 miles away in all directions; and this means, among other things, that strategic offensive rockets can be attacked during their ascent phase. Then again, there is no atmospheric scattering or absorption. This is of enormous benefit *vis-à-vis* streams of sub-atomic particles but also assists in respect of electromagnetic emissions.

Yet none of this means that beam weapons, be they particle or electromagnetic, can be made effective across whatever distance. As the very word implies, any form of 'radiation' is bound to spread out, the actual degree of divergence being directly proportional to its own wavelength though inversely proportional to the diameter of the projector being used. The result is a decrease in beam intensity with distance that is a function of the square of the range being registered. Say you treble the range. Then the intensity drops by eight-ninths.

Here it is important to stress that beams composed of particles are never exempt from this natural law. For in realms so peculiarly minute, assemblages of particles behave like waves, just as electromagnetic waves behave in part as assemblages of the primal parcels of energy known as photons. What is more, a stream of sub-atomic particles (electrons or whatever) can be produced only as a reaction against an electrical field. So not only will each and every one bear an electrical charge but, within a given beam, the charges in question will be either all positive or else all negative. Yet this must mean that they will repel one another, thereby markedly increasing their angular spread.

Therefore, both in the USA and, it seems, the USSR, beams composed of particles are a prospect held in less regard today than may have been the case five or ten years ago. Correspondingly, the development engineers in the former, at any rate, have already turned to the use of electromagnetic radiation to produce lethal concentrations of heat as photons are absorbed by a target. However, it is a matter of easy calculation that no such solution can be at all feasible unless the wavelengths employed are uniformly about as short as those of visible light, because they have been generated by lasers. Besides, feasibility is by no means the same thing as meeting the exacting canons of cost-benefit analysis. Suppose one makes studiedly sanguine assumptions about the power of the generators likely to be borne on laser battle-stations; about how wide the laser projectors themselves might be; and, above all, about the resistance to a concentrated heat influx of ascending enemy rockets. Even then, it is terribly hard to reckon up an orbital network of BMD, reliant on the lasering of visible light, without making it cost several (and perhaps many) times as much to create and sustain as the other side might spend on constructing enough extra missiles to swamp it.

To correct this imbalance, it would be necessary to develop lasers yielding waves of about X-ray length and therefore less prone to loss of concentration across long distances. But to progress to wavelengths as short as that would be to make a big and difficult leap forward, this because the electrons that a laser would have to energise for this purpose are ones revolving very close to the nuclei of their respective atoms.[3] Indeed, even laboratory research on X-ray lasering is still at an early stage. Therefore, this technique cannot conceivably be applied in the BMD stations President Reagan believes could be in Earth orbit by the turn of the century. At best, it would be manifest in a second-generation US system, from about the year 2010. Yet there are strong grounds for anticipating that, by then, the USSR will have narrowed or eliminated its lag in many branches of electronics; and continue developing ultra-long-range cruise-missiles, which are immune to beams from Space because they stay within the protective cover of the Earth's atmosphere throughout their flight.[4]

At all events, the Soviet Union will assuredly extend the capability it already has for intercepting Space vehicles in low orbit. What is more, if X-ray laser stations are to begin to satisfy the cost-benefit criterion referred to earlier, they will have to do so by operating over extended ranges. This is to say, they will have to be few in number, a circumstance that would much increase the exposure to crippling attrition of the network as a whole. Let us not forget, too, that every BMD station in orbit must individually be a lot more vulnerable than any rocket which suddenly and briefly ascends from the surface. Other facets which cannot be explored here include the problem of how to steer the beam with the accuracy required, the susceptibility to interference of the wireless links between the surface and the BMD station, and certain considerations within the spheres of arms control and alliance diplomacy. But enough has perhaps been said to confirm the point that neither the USA nor, of course, the USSR can hope to break their nuclear deadlock via this route. In other words, neither will ever be able to seek victory over its main adversary via the launching of an all-out nuclear war. For this reason alone, the popular notion that release of any nuclear warheads inevitably means the release of all of them everywhere appears as but a modern equivalent of medieval demonology.

Clearly, some of the connotations of continuing deadlock are benign. After all, in the early 1960s, a real and growing American superiority in this strategic nuclear sphere caused the Kremlin manifestly to be less at ease than it might otherwise have been, seeing that the bonnie if tarnished Nikita Khruschev was then premier and first secretary. One disturbing expression of this lack of composure was Marshal Malinovsky's explicit reintroduction of a doctrine of strategic nuclear pre-emption at the 1961 congress of the Communist Party of the Soviet Union. Another was Moscow's urgent attempt to emplace missiles in Cuba, in the autumn of 1962, in order to try and correct the developing imbalance. On the other hand, the new *status quo* is not without its sombre implications. There must, in principle, be a higher risk than before that a nuclear war would extend widely across Europe yet not over the border of the Soviet Superpower. Granted, this risk is diminished by the ghoulish futility of such a progression. Granted, too, it is lessened by the inescapable reality that much of the heavy fall-out from ground bursts in western Europe would be carried across the Soviet frontier on the westerly winds which blow so insistently at medium altitudes and above. But it may not be entirely obviated unless the Atlantic Alliance continues to provide for escalatory linkage through its nuclear doctrine and posture. One aspect of this provision is the maintenance of Intermediate-range Nuclear Forces in the European theatre. Another must be the retention by the USA of the option of Limited Strategic War as a way of forcing conflict termination.

Perhaps more serious as well as more centrally relevant to this study is this alternate possibility. A combination of (a) the objective reality of a nuclear stalemate between Washington and Moscow, and (b) doctrinal inhibitions against any first selective use of either theatre or strategic nuclear weapons would be conducive to non-nuclear fighting in Europe ramifying into a Limited World War. This is because the USSR, as the likely prime instigator of hostilities along these lines, might then little fear them sliding so far out of control as to culminate in nuclear strikes, including ones against herself. Undeniably, too, such a prospect of non-nuclear conflict involving the major powers is rendered all the more vexing by the pace at which the character of this kind of warfare is changing. Yet as was stressed in Chapter 1, nobody is in a position to dogmatise about the exact import of these changes.

The factors involved are diverse. Few lend themselves to simple extrapolation. Some, for example, do not lend themselves to enumeration of any kind. A few, like the weather and the calibre of individual leaders, are too random to figure definitively in a prognostic analysis. Others, for example sociology and physical geography, vary much with time and place.

Still, so long as all this is appreciated, it may be both possible and profitable to essay prediction of the shifting probabilities. Essentially two questions present themselves in relation to the 'no first use' debate. The first is whether the overall shift is in favour of defensive warfare, even when the two sides are well matched in quality. The second is whether, in the new technological environment, whatever technical ascendancy the West may continue to enjoy can be turned to decisive advantage. Looking then at the first issue, it is important to identify the broad characteristics of the technological revolution now under way. To an extent that would itself be remarkable by most previous experience, it takes the form of improvements in mobility. Metals and other materials have begun another surge forward in structural efficiency which means, above all, that vehicles can be made that much lighter, for a given task. Substantial savings in weight (or, alternatively, big advances in unrefuelled range) also accrue from the strides being made in the efficiency of fuel combustion. Moreover, these and other positive trends are being assisted by the use of computers to aid the design of vehicles as well as the actual operation of them and the weapons they bear. Even so, these gains in effective mobility are a minor theme in comparison with the advances in firepower now being achieved, principally through an extending exploitation of the electromagnetic spectrum coupled with the rapidly accelerating growth of computer science. An illustration may be taken from what might have been assumed to be quite a stable aspect of military applied science, namely, tank gunnery. In 1945, a stationary US battle tank had to fire its main gun a dozen times to stand a 50:50 chance of hitting the side of an adversary tank, positioned 2,000 metres down a test range. By 1975, a single round was enough to offer a better than 50:50 probability.[5]

Among other developments worth a mention here are two able to turn mobility into a source of vulnerability rather than a means of evasion. The discrimination of moving targets by means of Doppler radar is far from new but continues to get more proficient. Meanwhile, miniature mines, alias 'minelets', are coming into service which are so lethal yet compact that they may, for instance, readily be broadcast across an operational runway in order to render it unusable for a short yet maybe critical interval of time or be sown across or around a moving column so as to ensure that it further proceeds at its peril. Lastly, development has been started, both by the US Army and by the USAF, of sub-munitions that autonomously react to suitable targets and so home on them individually. Clearly, the rate of progress of the first generation of weaponry so novel and exotic must always be problematic. Even so, the likelihood now exists that, from the middle nineties, the concept in question will be widely implemented. Perhaps its most notable application will be when, as it descends, an artillery shell separates into several capsules, each able to guide itself onto a tank or some other 'hard-point' target. What this is tantamount to, of course, is the prospect that, so long as its general location is known beforehand, a mobile target can be aimed at individually without either the artillerist or anyone who is observing for him being in a 'line of sight' relationship with the target. This is almost the gunners' equivalent of the philosophers' stone.

Meanwhile, various of the new Precision-Guided Munitions (PGM) pose an added threat to fixed fortifications, minefields excepted. This is partly because accuracy rather than weight is usually the critical determinant of effectiveness against hard-point targets. More specifically, it is because between even the most solid of forts and the battlefield around, there have to be points of contact (embrasures, casements, periscopes, and antennae) which may be peculiarly susceptible to the phenomenal accuracy achieved by laser-ranging and guidance. Admittedly, it is hard to gauge how much relevance to West Germany this consideration has, bearing in mind the virtual proscription that obtains there against the erection of fixed defences ahead of a warlike crisis. But it certainly relates to other sectors of interest to the West: notably, eastern Turkey, the Golan and Korea. One respect in which both fire and movement are being assisted by electronics is improved surveillance by night. Thirty years ago, the most advanced aids available were clumsy infra-red emitters, devices all too prone to betray the whereabouts of those resorting to them. By the mid-1960s, however, image intensifiers relying just on ambient light were entering service. Now some even claim that, before very long, the aids to nocturnal vision will soon so improve that 'tanks, mechanized infantry and helicopters will be able to manoeuvre and engage the enemy at night as they can in the day'.[6] Though such claims do tend to be rather overpitched, progress in this sphere may well be sufficient to curb local probing and infiltration under cover of darkness. However, a more important effect will be to permit night-time attacks sufficiently heavy and frequent to make the Defence feel under presssure 'round the clock'. Not that the future battlefield will always be subject to full flows of data in all direction. Accidental interference is bound to occur. Much scope remains for deception. The active forms. of Electronic Warfare (jamming and attrition) may often compromise both communications and surveillance.

All the same, Electronic Warfare is unlikely to undermine the other side's surveillance and control capabilities completely, except as and when there is a large technology gap to exploit. Otherwise, the pattern will be patchy and erratic. At certain times, the data flow will lapse badly. But at others, it may be voluminous and definitive. Besides, the main electronic contribution to the increasing lethality of war is as indicated above, through advances in the accuracy of weapons delivery. These will not usually be too susceptible to interference, accidental, natural or deliberate.

However, the fashionable view that the potency of non-nuclear defence is markedly on the increase did not stem from an examination of electronic trends as such. Rather its origins lie in a thesis that the late Sir Basil Liddell Hart enunciated in 1960 with special reference to the European theatre.[7] It was that, ever since Napoleon's time, 'the Defence has been gaining a growing material ascendancy over the

Offence'.[8] He claimed this was a consequence of a steady fall in the number of troops needed to hold a mile of front in pitched battle, a fall due largely to continual improvements in firepower though also to a similarly positive trend in mobility and communications. Alas, this interpretation is wide open to objections. Not the least is that the only particular trend within the contemporary firepower revolution that Liddell Hart proved able to anticipate was the growing feasibility of night warfare; and even on this score, he conspicuously fails to observe the adverse connotations for the weaker side inherent in 'round-the-clock' combat. Yet the normal assumption is that this is the side which will be on the defensive. Nor did he recognise an even more fundamental distinction, that between light weapons and the heavier kinds of ordnance. The former are often carried and fired by individuals; mainly use solid shot; are often fired at a high rate in quite prolonged bursts; and are very generally aimed over 'open sights'. The latter are crew-manned; use explosive shells; and direct plunging fire against targets not visible to the gunners. Both elementary logic and a lot of historical experience indicate that improvements in the former will favour men resisting infantry and cavalry from prepared positions, whereas improvements in the latter do more to break those positions down.[9]

Besides, even if one could demonstrate that, in whatever may be the average case, the progress of firepower as such does favour the Defence, this could not guarantee its doing so in the context of more open warfare. Consider, for instance, the situation NATO's brigades and divisions in central Europe would face, unless heavily reinforced. The sectors they would have to cover would be abnormally wide, compared with most past experience. Therefore, they would be obliged to adopt a mobile pattern of defence, with much reliance on counter-attacks or fighting from prepared positions. Yet such advantages as may be peculiar to defensive warfare *per se* must relate in the main to more static deployment. A further complication is that posed by the 'square law' enunciated by F.W. Lanchester in 1916. What he said then was that 'the fighting strength of a force may be broadly defined as proportional to the square of its numerical strength, multiplied by the fighting value of its individual units'.[10] Granted, 'fighting value' is always hard to assess and quantify, especially in advance of actual conflict. Still, the import of his argument is that, when there is parity in value, even a fractional lead in numbers may hold out the promise of victory.

In the ultimate, this logical validation of the 'principle of mass' must hold good for every kind of military confrontation. However, it will the more readily be manifest when a formation can achieve something close to synoptic information about its adversaries, full contact with them, and a high 'kill-rate' per target engagement. Contrariwise, such factors as the concealment or inaccessibility of opposing forces retard the law's impact on the course of events. Historically speaking, the latter state of affairs has very often obtained in war, this not least in combat between armies. However, the electronic revolution promises to make the former more representative. Take, for example, the duels that so readily break out between opposing echelons of artillery. The backwards extrapolation of shell trajectories as tracked by radar now makes the location of enemy batteries a lot faster and more assured. Such technology can also facilitate the rapid correction of one's own fall of shot. For these and other reasons, attrition rates are likely to be considerably higher than before.

Not that we should be so bemused by such argument as to fall again, as per 1914, for 'the myth of the short war'. For when the respective sides are tolerably well matched substantively and in resolve, a more likely pattern may be as follows. A short though ferocious main battle is followed by an extended period of much less intense conflict or even uneasy truce; and this could, in its turn, be succeeded by one or more repetitions of a similar sequence. Needless to say, any period of stand-off would be considerably due to unprecedented physical wastage and psychological exhaustion; and hence an urgent need to recuperate, re-equip and reinforce. However, it might also owe much to (a) the economic and political repercussions of full-scale fighting, (b) the fear that such a situation might otherwise slide completely out of control and (c) what can fairly be inferred (as per Chapter 1) about the attraction the indefinite continuation of warfare could hold for the fascisto-Marxist wing of Kremlin opinion. Herein lies a powerful argument for keeping open various options of escalation in depth, including possible recourse to nuclear warheads. We must be able to force a cease-fire, rather than be obliged to accept an endless cycle of hostilities.

Nor is the specific prospect of brief yet savage main battles so very agreeable. All else apart, these could impose psychological shocks that short-term conscripts with no previous experience of war might find hard to withstand. Communist armies tend to be based on longer periods of full-time compulsory service than do conscripted forces in the West. Moreover, their imposition throughout of a harsh regime of discipline is further underpinned by the existence of a web of political informers and by such other factors as total control of the media. Evidently, too, psychological as well as material vulnerability would be at its most acute as and when offensive action began with a massive surprise attack. What has also to be remembered is that this stratagem (about which Liddell Hart was dismissive almost to the point of indifference) is one that is ever more menacing for other reasons. Among them is the likelihood that, in central Europe and certain other theatres, it will become harder to distinguish between a defensive adversary posture and an offensive one. This will be because of a shift away from the *blitzkrieg* stereotype whereby an offensive is narrowly focused on a chosen point of breakthrough. For concentrated assaults across open ground are liable to become as costly as they were between the advent of the machine gun and the invention of the tank. Accordingly, the standard scenario for the land battle is the more likely to be one fought across extended frontages with the principle of mass being applied not via convergence to effect a breakthrough but through the early commitment of more or less all available forces to a savage contest of attrition virtually the whole way along whatever line of contact geography allows.

Yet to observe this is to oblige oneself also to address what seems destined soon to become one of the most contentious issues in the whole defence debate: the future of the warplane, especially in hostile and well defended air space over the land. This is because the classic argument that only air power can concentrate swiftly enough around a point of decision, either to support the main armoured thrust or else to thwart it, is bound to count for less when there are not just one or two such foci. Likewise, reconnaissance well beyond the Forward Edge of the Battle Area (FEBA) will become less crucial when there is not the one thrust to identify, and if the enemy is less disposed to keep a high proportion of his ground combat formations grouped well to rearward, available for commitment as the battle reaches some climax in a focal sector. Nor are 'deep interdiction' strikes against lines of resupply and reinforcement as likely to prove profitable when those lines are well spread laterally and when there can be less reliance on reinforcement in the course of the main battle. Many analysts would insist, indeed, that enemy airfields are often the most tempting targets for deep strikes these days.

On the other hand, there are some respects in which tactical aircraft still seem considerably in the ascendant. Thus a strike fighter of today may well carry a warload equivalent to what a four-engined bomber could deliver in World War Two; and, of course, the modern ordnance will be far more lethal than before. Indeed, air ordnance is currently in a phase of particularly rapid development, this because it is deriving special benefit both from the latest advances in precision guidance and from new modes of warhead clustering. Now it is true to say that, for the first thirty years or so after World War Two, the improvements in warplane performance were bought at a considerable price. In other words, the cost of high-performance fighters and the like increased a lot faster than did inflation overall or the cost of other major types of weaponry. Since then, however, such divergence has much diminished. Take, for instance, the maximum speeds of manned interceptors. Between 1945 and 1965, these rose from around 0.6 on the Mach scale to 2.2.[11] But there they have broadly stayed, thus curbing cost escalation. This is because, if you do try to exceed Mach 2.2, you approach a major thermal barrier: a zone of much increased heat resistance that can be negotiated only through very heavy extra expenditure on development and construction. Besides which, the kind of speed here referred to may no longer be the most critical in air warfare. The rates of forward and lateral acceleration of the air-to-air missiles an interceptor fires may be more decisive. So may the alacrity of airborne computers.

To all of which may be added the way other trends alluded to earlier (the more efficient use of fuel; the advent of new structural materials; and the progressive miniaturisation of electronics) are facilitating reductions in overall weights and hence costs, performance for performance or task for task. Nor should one forget how much, in the field of aviation, this multiple evolution can benefit from a 'knock-on' effect. Thus the designs of modern fighter aircraft are so finely honed that, if the designers do directly save a pound in weight through any one of the various routes available, they end up saving another five or six pounds cumulatively. Nor, contrary to what is sometimes supposed, can it be said that tactical aircraft yet face rates of loss through enemy action significantly greater than was the case during, for instance, the closing stages of World War Two. For it would be fair to say that, in 1944-45, a representative spread of loss rates of aircraft would extend across the broad spectrum of between two and 30 for every 100 individual sorties. Yet it would be no less fair to say the same of our more recent experience.[12] Contrariwise, average attrition rates have already risen with various other types of weapons, tanks and artillery among them.

Nevertheless, the susceptibility of intruding aircraft to surface-to-air weapons has been drawing uncomfortably close to a most critical threshold in relation to the lowest heights and fastest speed acceptable in tactical flying; the consequent times of exposure over defended areas; and the quickening reactiveness even of such firmly established kinds of weapons as anti-aircraft guns and surface-to-air missiles. At the same time, certain interceptor aircraft are now fitted with missiles and electronics that enable them to engage low-flying intruders from above with much more assurance than before. Additionally, one should not rule out the possibility that the progressive development of lasers will eventually extend to their use as a means of short-range destruction (and especially surface-to-air destruction) as opposed to mere range-finding and target designation, their prime roles in warfare at present. As has just been implied, however, the pilots of intruding aircraft will not usually be able to offset the added threats from below and above by flying still faster and still lower. For should they attempt this, their own ability to play the part expected of them, that of active surveillance and flexible target acquisition, will tend to dwindle rapidly to zero.

So what has to be anticipated is an aggregation of trends that could soon lead to a sharp deterioration in the survival prospects for warplanes inside hostile air space. None the less, the various caveats ought to be entered, not least the following. As long as human beings stay directly involved in the control and operation of air defence, this will be strongly subject to a process of learning during the first few hours or even days of actual combat. Nor is there any sign of the said involvement being dispensed with entirely. All else apart, the thought of critical decisions about war being left entirely to 'robots' is ethically unappealing, throughout the West and also in the USSR. Yet taken in conjunction with the pronounced exposure of most manned aircraft nowadays to pre-emptive immobilisation on their own home base, the near-inevitability of an initial 'learning curve' lapse in the otherwise increasing potency of anti-aircraft defence has a disturbing implication. It is that aircraft may have to be characterised, more categorically than before, as instruments of 'first strike' in the context of non-nuclear theatre war. In other words, their changing fortunes will underline the argument that the attractions of surprise attack will grow.

In principle, of course, this particular tendency can be offset by increased reliance on other kinds of systems respectively to perform tasks today given more to warplanes. What has been said before about revolutionary types of artillery shell is one pointer in that direction. Another is a revived thrust towards longer range on the part of tubed artillery. Surface-to-surface missiles, unmanned reconnaissance planes, and satellites in orbit are other types of system that are able to make distinctive contributions. Nor should one forget that all these alternatives stand to benefit more than manned aircraft can from the trend in weight reduction. This is precisely because they do not have to transport crew members and their life-support systems. Even so, one has only to reflect on the slow and limited progress thus far made with the introduction of Vertical Take-Off and Landing monoplanes (meaning, at present, the three variants of the Harrier and the USSR's purely naval Yakolev-36) to appreciate how utopian it would be to expect the switch away from warplanes to be at all rapid. Nor may it be desirable for it ever to be at all complete. For one thing, it has long been recognised that strike aircraft are likely to retain better prospects for surviving and being effective when they are over the open sea, especially if they can be equipped with modern 'stand-off' weapons. For another, aircraft may come most into their own on land once a lot of attrition and dislocation has taken place all round: that is to say, towards the end of a main battle. Both then and beforehand, too, helicopters may have a bigger role to play than has been allowed them to date.

Overall, however, this brief review of the air dimension serves mainly to reinforce the conclusion that the technological trend in land or land-air warfare in a theatre like central Europe is in favour of the Offence: meaning, first and foremost, sudden and heavy surprise attack by the numerically superior side. This is essentially because the electronic revolution enables the logic of the Lanchester Square Law to be brought more directly to bear. Under these circumstances, explicitly to plan for a delay (perhaps indefinite) in the introduction of nuclear weapons into a European-style war could be tantamount either to an invitation to surprise attack or else to making one's own side alarmingly dependent on pre-emptive action. An obvious corollary is that, throughout a time of high political tension, there would be a severe risk of accidental war through misjudged pre-emption, certainly if nuclear deterrence had been cancelled out or played down. What is more, this risk would be much aggravated by a move towards more 'extended front' operations on land, making it that much harder to distinguish between preparations for Offence and those for Defence. Witness how, before the Yom Kippur war of 1973, the way the Egyptian army had deployed all along the Suez canal seriously compounded Israeli and American uncertainties about Cairo's intentions. No matter that on that particular occasion the actual decision went narrowly against pre-emption. What is more, far higher attrition rates on all sides would surely mean that more human and material resources would be needed to delay nuclear onset for a given time than is the case today. On that reckoning, the pressing question will be not whether to raise the nuclear threshold. It will be how to prevent it falling, a stark truth that comes to appear all the starker as one further reflects on the shock effect of suddenly imposing on young short-term conscripts with no prior combat experience, the awesome and ugly dynamic of the electronic battlefield.

Still, there is the one caveat to enter on the positive side. It is that the Soviet bloc does continue to lag technologically behind the industrial nations of the West. There is a general lag which often finds its most visible expression in lower levels of availability and, of course, reliability. But there is also a peculiarly acute lag in respect of electronics, one of its most dramatic manifestations to date being in the virtually unqualified ascendancy of the Israeli air force over the Syrian during the Lebanon war of 1982. Presumably, too, the inferiority the USSR and her allies labour under in this latter respect will be hard to correct so long as most aspects of the electronics revolution are at the middle stage of their curve of development, the stage of rapid and accelerating change. In other words, to be five years behind in 1990, say, may be far worse, substantively speaking, than it would have been in, say, 1960. Also, neither the institutional structure nor the pervading atmosphere of the Soviet Union itself may be well adapted to the advance of such exotic frontiers. The youthful enterprise and creativity that have come to characterise the 'silicon valleys' of the West cannot be easy for the tired revolution of Soviet Communism to emulate, not even in the 'scientific cities' that it has lately created.

Not that much complacency is warranted on this score. One factor that makes synoptic assessment and summation even harder than it usually is in such situations is that the quality of Soviet technology has long been remarkably variable, this even within such particular sectors as computing. Within many categories of weapon system, too, technology gaps are regularly less pronounced (and likely to matter less in any case) than with, to take one of the most extreme examples, the electronics of air superiority fighters. Even with surface-to-air defence, indeed, a defender's capabilities may have to be judged more in relation to the basic tasks of tracking and interception than in relation to the specific capabilities of the adversary air force. A close analogy can, of course, be drawn with what has been said earlier about the interception of battle stations in Space. Besides, it would be rash to jump to conclusions about the extent of the West-versus-Soviet gap even ten years hence, bearing in mind our poor track record, since 1945, of prediction in this area. What can and must be said, however, is that various kinds of electronic change may successively be slowing down during the 1990s, as this revolution as a whole approaches maturity. If so, the Communists will be afforded an opportunity to catch up from behind. Neither should we forget that, in this sphere as in others, the Communists can do a lot to compensate for qualitative lag by larger (and maybe more diverse) inventories or by faster rates of replacement. Moreover, it may be more successful than the West in the illicit obtaining of Electronic Intelligence, a factor of growing tactical importance.

It may be, too, that COMECON (the multilateral institution that overviews the economics of the Soviet bloc) will prove tolerably effective in regard to the international division of tasks in advanced electronics and related technologies. Undeniably, some of what the West gains from creative enterprise it loses from duplication. Nor is it yet clear to what extent the exceptional potential of Japanese electronics can and will be mobilised for the benefit of Western defence. Nor should we ever forget that the Communist policies have various features that might enable them to sustain certain patterns or belligerency better; and that these features do not become less relevant in the light of the military-technical revolution discussed above. Prominent among them are complete governmental control over the media; a secret police; relatively long periods of conscription; and pre-induction military training. Even in the realms of military science as narrowly defined, indeed, armed forces that are either Soviet or modelled very much on Soviet lines may be singularly well adapted, in certain important respects, to changing needs. Thus Soviet distaste for elaborated philosophies of command and control could prove more apposite than some in the West might care to think, in a military environment characterised by extended frontages, rapid attrition and recurrent electronic chaos. Likewise, the time-honoured Russian emphasis on artillery may well be coming back into its own, as both tanks and aircraft become more vulnerable. Nor is this all. The USSR's disinclination to see supply trains grow at all large may be less out of place in the future than it has been in the recent past. Meanwhile, her concern to be able markedly to expand or reconstitute forces-in-being may be of growing relevance. Indeed, even her problems *vis-à-vis* serviceability may be of less consequence if main battles are liable to be of short duration.

Admittedly, it is hard to gauge how much substance there may be in the argument, fashionable again of late, that 'the Russians never throw away' discarded weapons. But if they do stockpile old equipment at all prodigiously, this could also stand them in good stead during a phase of competitive reinforcement. After all, certain margins of inferiority associated with older models of weapons may matter less in the future than in the recent past, the maximum speeds of mobile platforms (surface or aerial) not infrequently being a salient case in point. Also, increasing recourse to modular replacement is facilitating the updating of individual weapons systems. To an extent, too, manifold advances in ordnance mean that the limits on total performance will be determined more within a weapon itself and less within its delivery platform.[13]

All of which suggests that tactical nuclear dissuasion has a needful part to play in underpinning the defence preparations of the West and its allies. For would not any Soviet commander invading, say, Bavaria be inhibited by the knowledge that the further his troops advanced the greater was the risk of nuclear warheads coming into play? And would not his Western opposite number be sustained by an awareness that his efforts could, if successful, prevent an escalation to nuclear war? The answer to all these questions has to be a strong affirmative, even though a possibility does exist that a hope of eliminating some of their opponents' theatre nuclear weapons could incline some of the Warsaw Pact's elite formations towards more offensive vigour. Suffice here to observe a predictable yet most disturbing paradox. Those who advocate 'no first use' or 'higher thresholds' are often the very people who would circumscribe the martial art and dilute the martial virtues. They are those who would seek proscriptions on other 'cruel weapons', like napalm.[14] They are those who press for full access, licit or otherwise, to defence information; for conscientious objection to military service or combat duty being accepted as the most available of rights; for military trade unions; for sex equality in the armed services; and for curbs on hierarchical distinctions within them. Moreover, their concern is rarely with whether any such reforms would be conducive to military cohesion and resolve. Rather it is with what they see as the moral imperative of making military service conform as closely as possible to the norms of a permissive and hedonistic civil society. By the same token, they would be either indifferent or hostile to any endeavours to prepare our society for the rearward support, moral and material, of any war effort that may be called for. And yet, notionally at least, they stand prepared to ask of young men and maybe women that they be ready to fight in wars that might drag on indefinitely but which could sometimes (and especially at their outset) evince a pace and savagery far worse than anything experienced at, say, Anzio or in Normandy.

CHAPTER FOUR

THE CENTRAL EUROPEAN THEATRE

Note has often been taken of the concern shown by the Kennedy administration to augment NATO's non-nuclear strength in Europe. What has largely been overlooked, however, is that during those years (1961-63) the number of US nuclear warheads located in that theatre more than doubled to 7,000, their combined explosive yield being officially adjudged to exceed 400 megatons: over 100 times what Allied bombers had dropped on the Third Reich between 1939 and 1945. In the interim, a few hundred British and French nuclear devices have also become available.

As regards individual warhead types, the lowest on the scale of nuclear explosive yield have been those used in certain US demolition charges or air-to-air missiles. For their detonation corresponds to a mere one or two hundred tons of TNT. Towards the higher end have been the Pershing IA surface-to-surface ballistic missiles in service with the US Army and the Bundeswehr. Each releases up to 400 kilotons, having travelled up to 450 miles. However, many of the 1,250 nuclear bombs available for aerial delivery, as of 1981, were in the megaton range.[1] Moreover, many of these were and are assigned to warplanes (such as the Phantom or F-111) able to essay quite deep penetration of the USSR.

Then, in December 1979, NATO Council confirmed plans to have the USA deploy on European soil 464 BGM-109A Ground-Launched Cruise Missiles (GLCM) and 108 Pershing IIs. The former travel up to 1,400 miles and the latter up to 1,200. Among the warloads a Pershing II can carry is a warhead capsule with five individual charges of perhaps 75 kilotons apiece. Now, of course, deployment has actually begun. All the Pershings are destined for Germany while the GLCMs will go to Britain, the Low Countries and Italy[1] But at that same Council meeting, NATO decided to offset this new departure by effecting a net reduction of one thousand in the total number of warheads (those for GLCM and Pershing II included) in the European theatre; and the requisite withdrawals are now complete. Furthermore, it was agreed in the autumn of 1983 that another 1,400 warheads should be removed over the next few years.

This double decision has essentially been an outcome of studies that have been going on ever since theatre nuclear modernisation was first revived as an issue in 1977. The indications[2] are that these have been favouring a substantial cutback in warheads designed for more localised use: the demolition charges, artillery shells etc. The main reason would appear to be doubts about whether, in the context of ever more dynamic war, the systems in question would be at all suitable as instruments of controlled nuclear release. But this revaluation may also betoken the final abandonment of any notion that nuclear firepower might be used to win a European war, as opposed to forcing a halt in it. On both counts, the sanguineness of the Kennedy-McNamara era has implicitly been renounced. In other respects, however, the doctrinal and institutional bases of NATO nuclear strategy are the same as before. Still prominent among the doctrines is the commitment to a Forward Strategy for deterrence and defence in Germany. So, too, is the precept that any recourse to nuclear (or chemical) weapons must be subject to overriding political control, this to be exercised essentially by the following parties: the government within whose territory release will take place; that whose troops will effect it; and the President of the United States. Moreover, these operative authorities would be required to act in accordance with guidelines laid down by NATO's Defence Planning Committee and Council of Ministers: this most particularly in the light of successive recommendations by a Nuclear Planning Group (NPG) established in 1967. Its seven national members routinely meet in ministerial session twice a year.

From 1960 onwards, General Laurie Norstad, Supreme Allied

Commander Europe between 1956 and 1963, enunciated what also became a key element in the planning for contingent nuclear introduction. This was the precept that the nuclear capabilities then being made organic to the major formations 'could, if the situation demands, be joined promptly and effectively with the conventional effort to force a pause' for what hopefully would be constructive crisis bargaining.[3] In other words, limited nuclear firepower might be introduced into a battle situation in order to achieve concurrently two quite different objects: obtaining a tactical dividend (e.g. the destruction of a bridge) and betokening a wider political and military resolve. Yet to note this may be to indicate how certain particularities of strategy ought still to be critically addressed. To mix aims thus could be ineluctably to undermine the authority of the politicians over the military in that any decision would have to hinge largely on the inflow of military information and the professional interpretation thereof. Besides which, to explode one or two nuclear warheads within a congested battle zone would perforce be to risk a heavy counterstrike in kind. Perhaps, too, this risk would be aggravated by the way 'forward defence' requires virtually every brigade and division under NATO command to deploy for war within a few miles of the inter-German border. Also, it must be said, by a visibly heavy reliance on strike aircraft as providers of a regional deterrent against such escalation. The crowding of such machines onto a limited number of airfields in exposed locations may invite escalation rather than deter it.

What then of Warsaw Pact theatre nuclear doctrine? The first point to make is that it is suffused with Clausewitzian perceptions (as per Chapter 2) but, above all, dominated by Soviet military perspectives; and, during this last decade or so, this domination has carried with it a high regard for the dividends to be derived from sudden and massive offensive action. Indeed, such action is seen as continuing to clear-cut victory even within the context of the actual or threatened use of theatre nuclear weapons. At the same time, what one can discern of the theatre nuclear posture of the Warsaw Pact confirms the strong influence of continentalist scepticism about the exact modulation of nuclear release. Granted, nuclear artillery shells with yields in the order of one kiloton are available down to divisional level in Ground Forces Soviet Germany (GFSG). But it is likely that a Soviet division – on a war establishment – still holds fewer nuclear warheads than does a NATO one; and a similar comparison can be drawn on the air side. Moreover, there has to date been no evidence of the USSR aligning nuclear warheads with the armed forces of its East European allies though, of course, the states in question do possess aircraft and missiles that could be armed thus.

So suppose one assumes that there are theatre nuclear stockpiles earmarked for crisis distribution to other Warsaw Pact members. Then such analysis as can be conducted points to a total which has lately risen yet is still rather below NATO's five to six thousand. However, an added complication has been that, as the Soviets amassed a panoply of a strategic nuclear weapons, they gave a quite extraordinary priority to retaliation against Europe rather than North America. Thus between 1961 and 1963, no fewer that 600 Intermediate-or-Medium-range Ballistic Missiles (IRBMs/MRBMs) were deployed to this end inside the western borders of the USSR. Yet this was at a time when the Intercontinental Ballistic Missile (ICBM) force – located deep in the Soviet heartland and targetted on the USA – was only creeping past the fifty mark. Indeed, this misplaced 'Euro-emphasis' largely explains both the origin and the outcome of the Cuba crisis of 1962. Moscow had put itself in some danger of actually being defeated in a strategic exchange with North America.

What is more, the anxiety induced (especially in West Germany) by the Muscovite preoccupation with Europe was to be recharged in the seventies by the advent and progressive deployment of two large and strikingly exotic delivery vehicles: the Tupolev-22M 'swing-wing' bomber (code-named Backfire by NATO) and the SS-20, a land-mobile IRBM which fires with precision three warheads of perhaps 150 kilotons yield apiece. The former entered service in 1974 and the latter in 1977. Nearly half the 400 IRBMs and MRBMs currently located in the West of the USSR are SS-20s. Alongside them, speaking broadly, stand perhaps 300 medium-range strategic bombers, a good third of which will be Backfires as of August

1984. To which must be added the complication that, as from early 1984, SS-22 missiles (range, 600 miles) have been deployed in East Germany.

Turning from nuclear weapons to chemical ones is customarily seen as a natural progression. Unfortunately, however, it leads one to a sphere of pronounced Warsaw Pact ascendancy, certainly on the offensive side. Only the two Superpowers plus France have offensive capabilities at all. The Soviet stockpile is put at 300,000 tons and growing. Its US counterpart is much smaller and becoming obsolescent. Production stopped in the USA some 15 years ago. Resumption has been considered but continues to face strong domestic opposition, not least on Capitol Hill.

Looking at conventional forces according to the latest edition of *The Military Balance*, the armies of NATO have 27 active divisions or division equivalents in West Germany and the Low Countries. Twelve of these are Bundeswehr; five American; four from the Low Countries; three British; and three French. There is also a Canadian brigade.

Quite the weightiest contribution on the Warsaw Pact side of the central area (East Germany, Czechoslovakia, and Poland) is Ground Forces Soviet Germany (GFSG). For a good quarter of a century, their divisional order of battle was kept at 20. Late in 1979, however, one tank division was withdrawn, apparently to help indicate that an imminent incursion into Afghanistan was not intended as the opening round in World War Three. Meanwhile, two more Soviet divisions continue to cover lines of communication through Poland, while the five-division Soviet garrison established in Czechoslovakia in 1968 also remains. As regards indigenous forces, there are six East German Divisions, ten Czech and fifteen Polish. In other words, the Warsaw Pact standing armies in this all-important central area have a divisional advantage of two to one. Then how, one might ask, do such imbalances relate to what appears as the much less acute one apropos the number of soldiers with the colours: 800,000 with NATO and 1,000,000 with the Warsaw Pact?

One explanation of the seeming contradiction is that, whilst the indigenous Warsaw Pact divisions are at varying levels of readiness, their average manning level is barely half their wartime establishment. More fundamentaly, however, Soviet-style divisions are less elaborately structured than are their Western counterparts, relatively rich though the former may be in such basic factors as tanks and artillery. So it is that the nominal roll of a complete Soviet tank division is some 12,000 men, where that of its US counterpart is more likely to be 17,000. What is more, when acount is also taken of the number of troops required behind each division for logistic and other rearward duties, the respective calculations become 20,000 and 40,000. Still, all this affords but a first approximation to the regional military balance. The Warsaw Pact members continue collectively to derive not inconsiderable dividends, in terms of flexibility and economy, from a greater standardisation of organisation and equipment. They benefit, too, from the long periods of army conscription, between eighteen months and two years as compared with the eight to fifteen months that are currently operative in the relevant member countries of NATO.[4] Contrariwise, however, four of NATO's members (Britain, Canada, Luxembourg and the USA) now have no compulsory service whatsoever. Armies composed of long-service volunteers do, as a rule, reach higher standards of training and group cohesion. On the other hand, they generate much thinner echelons of recallable reserves.

No such overview could be deemed at all complete unless some attention were paid to the air dimension. Here the most fundamental reality to reackon with is the sheer weight of tactical aviation permanently available to each side. Comparison can instructively be made with the *blitzkrieg* phase of the Second World War, an era in which warplanes served only too effectively to spherahead mechanised attack against troops mostly lacking, like their counterparts today, prior experience of war. In their campaign across the mountainous and maritime flanks of Europe (Scandinavia and the Balkans) the Germans did employ what would still be regarded as a high proportion of air power. However, in the big overland campaigns against the Low Countries and France in 1940 and then the USSR in 1941, the Luftwaffe had only 20 to 25 aeroplanes committed for every army division the

Wehrmacht had deployed. The corresponding ratio within central Europe today is about 65 in NATO and about 55 in the Warsaw Pact. Not that these figures tell anything like the whole story. They take no acount of the huge expansion in the number of aircraft (meaning, most particularly, the many hundreds of helicopters) operated by the armies themselves. Nor do they allow for the much bigger part surface weapons play today in air defence. Nor the ability of hundreds of modern warplanes to sortie over the central area from bases in Britain, France, Spain and, of course, the USSR.[5] Nor is account taken of the marked technical evolution of warplanes, as regards both size and performance.

Evidently, NATO continues to enjoy an advantage over the Warsaw Pact in various of the qualitative aspects of tactical air power. What is uncertain, however, is whether this edge would find expression in one of the most critical comparisons of all: the relative frequency with which aircraft would sortie. Granted, several of the differences which can be observed or inferred as between the respective air fleets could lead one to the conclusion that, for some years ahead at least, the sortie rates the Warsaw Pact might register in a central European war would fall well below those of NATO. These relate to the provision of electronics aids for nocturnal and all-weather flying; the size of the ground support staff, military and civilian; the ancillary equipment (not least flight simulators) available on base; and the pattern and intensity of peacetime flying training. Even so, a 1976 analysis by a staff member of the Arms Control and Disarmament Agency in Washington credited the Warsaw Pact with a sortie rate 20 per cent superior to NATO's.[6] It might be best to view this in relation to other American admonitions that NATO was not yet paying as much attention as was the Warsaw Pact to a surge capability within the not unlikely context of a short, highly dynamic war.

So how readily might aerial reinforcements arrive for the 1,700 NATO and 3,100 Warsaw Pact warplanes currently in service in central Europe? Salient among those on which NATO is reliant are the 50 or so squadrons (approximately 1,000 planes) that the US Air Force could deploy from across the Atlantic within 10 days. Until recently, the situation on the

Soviet side was as follows. Just over half the air armada operational within Soviet borders (some 5,600 machines as of 1980) were earmarked for the tactical support of the 150 or so Soviet army divisions of the line that were also home-based. So assuming that the warplanes in this echelon would move into central Europe at a rate closely corresponding to the inflow of land forces, it seemed fair to say that something over half of the three thousand aircraft in question would arrive in the central European theatre inside one month.

What then of the other echelon: the 2,600 or so planes in PVO-Strany, the independent air command formally tasked with the comprehensive defence of the homeland against an air onslaught or aerial infiltration? For some time, some of us had been assuming that the authorities in Moscow had already recognised that preparations thus to resist any very heavy attack by manned bombers had lost much of their relevance now that the strategic deterrent forces of the West were predominantly in the form of long-range missiles. Accordingly, our expectation was that the elite command in question would be considerably available for deployment abroad (meaning, above all, central Europe), in the event of a warlike confrontation. Contrariwise, a 1974 study sponsored by the Brookings Institution drew the conclusion that such diversion was improbable.[7] But today there can be no doubt that these resources are, in fact, available for despatch to Germany or elsewhere. Various indications that institutional provision is being made for this have been discernible since 1981. Some interchange has been taking place between PVO-Strany and the Soviet air force proper in regard to the filling of senior command posts. Meanwhile, within PVO-Strany itself, the dichotomy has sharpened between the command structure for interceptor aircraft and that for surface-to-air missiles. Already it is clear, indeed, that a vast reorganisation of Soviet air power is underway, fully involving both PVO-Strany and 'frontal aviation'. The assets in question have been regrouped into just five tactical air armies: their respective headquarters being in Irkutsk, Legnica (in Poland), Moscow, Smolensk, and Vennitsa. Apparently, the 24th tactical air army in the German Democratic Republic has ceased to exist as such. Nor is it at all certain that PVO-Strany as a whole will retain a distinct identity. Relating this trend to the long-standing integration of the command and control of air defence as between the USSR and the rest of the Warsaw Pact, one has to conclude that Moscow has made nearly all its home-based aviation available to reinforce local theatres in Europe and elsewhere. Over and beyond which, there has long been little dispute that (save for the nuclear backcloth) the Warsaw Pact enjoys a commanding advantage in terms of army reinforcement, especially during the first weeks of high tension. For one thing, each and every division in the East German, Czech and Polish armies could soon be raised to battle strength. For another, GFSG could be boosted by an estimated 40 divisions within a month, this capability being the product of the overland network of transport links and of there being some 80 divisions (perhaps 30 or 35 of them at an advanced state of preparedness) in European Russia, exclusive of Caucasia.

Obversely, the USA with Canada could only fly or sail some six or seven divisions across the North Atlantic within the same timespan, even if there were no interference with the said movement. And as regards the possibility of interference, one is bound to observe that nowhere has Soviet maritime power built up more strongly of late than in that ocean basin; and also that the said build-up now poses at least some threat to the Allied airlift as well as to transit by sea. So allowing that the equivalent of about two divisions would be arriving from Britain and very possibly, several from France, one has to say this. Even if allied movements were not impeded by enemy action or internal politics, the military balance in central Europe would tilt a lot more against NATO over the first three or four weeks of competitive military reinforcement associated with some East-West political crisis. Not surprisingly, a new official study has come to similar conclusions about the European theatre as a whole.[8] The differential in question is partly a function of the size of the Warsaw Pact's *masse de manoeuvre*. But it derives more fundamentally from the geographical parameters of strategic mobility, especially as respectively applied to the Superpowers (see Chapter 1).

Here, surely, is a major dilemma for the advocates of 'no first use'. For they always aver or assume, however misguidedly, that all they have to do to round off their argument is demonstrate that something close to a non-nuclear equivalence could always be preserved throughout any military confrontation in Germany. What is more, all such soldierly concerns are made the more pertinent by the likelihood that the European political scene will become more stressful in due course. After all, the USSR is sure to find the rest of Eastern Europe harder to control as time goes by. Yet she will also find her control harder and harder to relinquish. For she believes too obsessively in the 'domino theory', as applied to the infectious appeal of liberalisation spreading out of Western Europe through Eastern Europe and into herself. The central place that Europe continues to occupy in Moscow's strategic concerns these days owes far more to this historic fear than it does to the alternative one of military attack.

At the same time, however, Western Europe may find its political equilibria threatened more insistently by economic weakness than has been the case since the forties: this is to say, since the confidence injected by Marshall Aid raised non-Communist Europe above the slough of despond it had nearly collapsed into in 1947 and 1948. For its old industrial heartlands will be beset by economic perils. One of them will be sluggish or erratic growth in the international economy as a whole. Yet paradoxically enough, another will be ever more intense industrial competition from overseas, this within the context of rapid technological innovation. The implications for European peace and security are unlikely to be positive. Yet even in the absence of such instabilities, Europe would remain what it has so often been – a theatre into which menacing tensions may readily extend from warlike crises elsehwere.

CHAPTER FIVE

THE WIDER COMPASS

A saddening aspect of the 'peace movement' is the way its obsessively anti-nuclear stance atrophies certain of the more positive elements within the world view of some who lend it their support. Historically speaking, there has been a strong perception on the Left that we live in 'one world' in regard to the upholding of international law; economic management; and the drive against poverty, prejudice and tyranny. What is more, the biggest single impulse behind this global formulation has come from a conviction that 'peace is indivisible'.

Alas in 1984, the preconditions of general peace as thus identified are as far from realisation as ever. Even the most workaday aspects of international law are seriously under threat, even from established governments. Witness the repeated submarine intrusions into Swedish territorial waters, the Iraqi use of poison gases in the Gulf War, the killing of South Korean ministers in Rangoon, Libya's sinister corruption of diplomatic immunity, and Bulgaria's attempt to assassinate the Pope. Poverty still abounds, not least in the mushrooming cities of the developing world. Prejudice and tyranny are almost commonplace. Indeed, not a few of the more crucial political, economic and ecological trends are as negative as ever. Evidently, this state of affairs could much encourage the wide escalation of any warlike crisis in which the USSR and West are involved at all directly (see Chapter 2). To take the argument back a stage, the frequency with which warlike crises erupt in one region or another seems bound to remain high. Almost by definition, the actual course of such events hardly lends itself to even approximate prediction. None the less, certain patterns of probability can be outlined. First and foremost, one has to say that the broad arc of South-West Asia from Turkey through to India (lately identified by this author as 'Near East Major'[1]) is a region which invites singular concern. It is a part of the world in which even the Superpowers find it exceptionally hard to control their clients or even (as evidenced by the agonisings in Moscow and Washington about the Gulf War) to determine whom they may wish to regard as clients. It stands comparison with central Europe in terms of the aggregation of armaments, nuclear warheads excepted. It is steadily generating the technical prerequisites for considerable nuclear proliferation. Several of its member countries control enough short-term credit to destabilise at a stroke the international monetary system. It is a zone of intense cultural turmoil. The endless race war between Israeli Jew and Palestinian Arab torments the political and religious psyche of the West, not least that of the United States. It has witnessed, in Afghanistan, quite the biggest single military intervention the USSR has effected since 1945.

Then ignoring the vast deposits of unduly heavy oil off the Orinocan coast of Venezuela, it is still adjudged to contain over half the proven oil reserves of this planet; and the production costs of its contribution to world output (just under 30 per cent at present) remain remarkably low. On this account alone, one cannot but deplore the disposition of some Americans to rejoice most visibly at how their country has virtually freed itself from direct reliance on petroleum imports from 'Near East Major' so far as the immediate future is concerned. But another compelling reason for regarding this celebration as misguided is that Western Europe and Japan are among the many areas that cannot escape, even a while, from their reliance on oil from this quarter. Were either or both ever to collapse into Marxian revolution on account of energy starvation, the outlook for all Mankind (the USA most certainly included) would become grim. Just a part of the justification for saying this has to be that such a development would be strongly conducive to a rebuilding of a Moscow-Peking axis.

Among the less agreeable possibilities is the formation

sometime these next few years of a radical Left axis extending from Tehran through Baghdad to Damascus or even Beirut. Not that such a conjunction is immediately in prospect. To take first the internal situation in Iran, the Communists (as per the Tudeh party) have been de-legitimised and all but broken; the conservatives are ascendant within the religious leadership; and the army remains of some account in the public domain. Yet irrespective of the approaching demise of Ayatollah Khomeini or of the possibility of an acute economic crisis affecting Iran, valid enough grounds exist for apprehending a Marxian revival in association with the radical mullahs: the alliance of the 'Reds' and the 'Blacks' about which the late Shah used to warn the West. All else apart, it is evident that, the armed forces partially excepted, the Iranian revolution has been devastatingly successful at sweeping away the institutional infrastructure of the old order. In other words, it has deprived counter-revolution of a matrix within which to flourish. Correspondingly, it has created a quasi-vacuum in which the intellectual lumber of Marx and the cellular structure extolled by Lenin might quite readily be implanted.

As and when the government of Saddam Hussein falls in Baghdad, there may simply be a realignment of power among Iraq's military chiefs and Ba'athist politicians. However, an acute economic crisis could so interact with resentment over the Gulf War as to precipitate some more fundamental shift. This could hardly be in the direction of Islam, if only because the Iraqi Shi'ites lack the necessary impetus. So it would most likely be towards the anti-Western Left, at least in respect of external policies. Clearly, this could be conducive to a reconciliation with Syria. All of which renders it only too easy to imagine situations in which at least the threat of military intervention became a Western imperative; above all, to preclude oil starvation through a wilful witholding of exports or else because the supply network was being ravaged as an unchecked consequence of violent regional conflict. Unfortunately, the realisation that such a response was imperative would not *ipso facto* make it feasible. Instead, it is also too easy to think of circumstances in which intervention would prove decidedly unfeasible unless the option of Limited Strategic War or some other pattern of nuclear escalation was being kept open.

When one talks of force projection by the West to the Gulf, what one has in mind above all else is the dispatch of the Rapid Deployment Joint Task Force (RDJTF), organised by the Pentagon since the Iranian revolution. Yet even in the course of what might be a profoundly fateful five weeks, the RDJTF could muster in the Gulf a mere two-and-a-half divisions.[2] That is to be compared with the Soviet order of battle in Transcaucasia, Turkestan and Afghanistan: no less than 20 divisions, a significant proportion of which could deploy across the Iranian border. It might also be compared with the 24 in the orders of battle of Iran and Iraq.[3] Even allowing that the American formations would be of exceptional strength and quality and that a combination of politics and logistics would always ensure that they would never have to do battle with more than a minor fraction of such adversary forces, the disproportions disconcert.

Nor is this the only factor that potentially operates on the negative side. Considerable provision would probably have to be made as well for air cover and, of course, for routine replenishment to the tune of (in conditions of heavy combat) several thousand tons a day. Furthermore, nobody dare wax complacent about the willingness and ability of the air arms and other forces of friendly indigenous powers to shield the ports and airfields through which the RDJTF and supporting elements might arrive. Another constraint to reckon with, one that could render necessary a much longer period of grace than the five weeks cited above, is denial of the privilege of overflight. Additionally or alternatively, there may be active interference with the air and sea lanes in question. The exceptional difficulties posed by operations in the Gulf is epitomised by one of its strongest singularities: the unmatched strain of acclimatisation imposed in high summer on troops airlifted in from temperate climes.[4]

Still, at least there is a general awareness within public opinion in the West that 'Near East Major' (and the Gulf, in particular) has menacing possibilities. Witness the broad endorsement of the moves the USA made this last summer to deter a widening of the Iraq-Iran war. But on the other side of Asia, another most dangerous focus of political antagonism and military confrontation, that across the Korean peninsula, goes largely unremarked. Yet nothing seen on this Earth to date bears more resemblance to *Nineteen Eighty-Four* than the way the pair of authoritarian regimes in North and South Korea perennially invoke the horrors of each other in reciprocal self-justication. Having said that, there is something uniquely sinister about North Korea. How can a Communist President anoint his 'even wilder-eyed' son[5] as his heir? Has the whole of the post-war era witnessed any ploy more nasty than that assassination through bombing of the four South Korean government ministers along with thirteen other South Koreans (this almost certainly by North Korean agents) in Rangoon in October 1983. Was there a connection between this incident and the shooting down the previous month of the Korean airliner, an event many of us initially took to have been a macabre but authentic accident?

Granted, the avid claims of South Korea to be part of the 'free world' are vitiated by its system of government continuing to be decidedly illiberal. What is more, its stability is ultimately placed at risk thus, as evidenced by the way nearly 200 were killed in the apparently spontaneous uprising against political repressiveness which took place in the town of Kwangju in 1980. But the prospects of progressive relaxation will not be enhanced if South Korea's resolve to defend herself against aggression is not properly underwritten. Furthermore, the abandonment of that policy would (a) demoralise Japan deeply and (b) strongly encourage a realignment of Moscow and Peking. All else apart, the endeavours regularly made by Pyongyang (the North Korean seat of government) to effect the latter consummation would gain extra impetus and influence. By some criteria, the 1953 armistice line between the two Koreas does appear quite a secure defensive front. Man-made fortifications considerably reinforce the strength of the natural topography. The ratio of forces in being to sectoral width would be a lot more favourable for a South Korea faced with an all-out attack than, to draw the obvious comparison, for NATO in West Germany. As things stand, too, the South

Koreans show every sign of being willing enough to fight.

Even so, it would be quite wrong to infer that nuclear weapons have no part to play in deterrence and defence in the peninsula. Here the first point to make is that, whatever the intrinsic pros and cons, the mere process of moving from the *status quo*, with its implicit nuclear backing to the general American commitment, to a 'no first use' stance could be destabilising. Early in 1950, the late Dean Acheson inadvertently paved the way for the Korean War (which, in fact, broke out that June) by publicly declaring, in his capacity as Secretary of State, that South Korea lay outside the 'defense perimeter' of the United States. Were one of his successors to announce that henceforward the said republic was effectively beyond the 'nuclear umbrella' of the United States, their words would similarly be read both sides of the armistice line as betokening an overall lessening of concern on Washington's part in respect of the peninsula, particularly since the said decision presumably would involve the actual withdrawal of the several 100 warheads currently held by the US garrison in the South.[6] Such a reading would do nothing for the resolve of the South or the docility of the North. This eventuality apart, there is bound always to be some risk of the South's being overwhelmed by a sudden offensive, given that Seoul (its political capital and booming centre of industry) stands only forty miles from what would be the North Korean start line. Then looking ahead, one has to allow, too, that falling birth rates along with pressure for reduced conscription (currently a minimum of 30 months) will make it harder to sustain a military establishment of over 600,000 men. Nor are the maritime approaches ever entirely secure. Most importantly, however, the very fact that the border zone is manned each side by strong garrisons means that an adventurist regime in Pyongyang can essay local actions with a confident awareness that any fighting thus brought about does not have to escalate into all-out hostilities. Many such probes were made, principally by the North, in the last year before the outbreak of the 1950-3 war. Many more were made, against the background of a military stalemate, across the waist of the peninsula, during the last two years of that conflict. Quite a number more have been made by the North since, though never on a grand scale, like the Rangoon assassination.

What would be totally unacceptable is the generation and indefinite continuation of a bolder and more intensive probing campaign. The point merits stressing because, against a background of a US declaratory commitment to 'no first use', such a departure could be highly attractive to the fascisto-Marxists of Pyongyang. It would help them to preserve their monolithic grip on their own people. It would preclude the evolution in South Korea of a more liberal environment. Otherwise, however, such an evolution is (a) feasible because, though the South is authoritarian, it is also pluralist and (b) needful because South Korea is now, politically and culturally, well within the ambit of Western influence and aspirations. Indeed, it is not unfair to surmise that one reason why Pyongyang has not adopted so tough a strategy to date is that the United States might eventually resort to the selective use of low-yield nuclear weapons in order to block an endeavour to collapse the Republic of Korea by thus generating a crisis in its political development. Meanwhile, the brittle fragility of the strategic balance in that part of the world is further revealed by a cursory glance at the military relationship between the Japanese archipelago and the USSR. The sector in question is of vital (and, indeed, rising) importance to the Soviets, not least in respect of the operation of what the Americans call FBMs, those submarines dedicated to the firing of nuclear missiles (Chapter 3). Yet the naval and related facilities in question are remarkably constricted by geography. Contrariwise, the sheer weight of physical force (nuclear weapons apart) is heavily on the side of the Soviets. In other words, they could readily pose a grave threat to a country that has a most important part to play in the progress of Western democracy.

Oddly enough, exactly the same things have to be said about the relationship between northern Norway and the contiguous parts of the USSR.[7] So neither of these sectors should be ignored by anybody reflecting on whether we can base our global strategy on such a precept as 'no first use'. Nor should the involuted complexities of 'Near East Major'. Nor are these the only contingent *casi belli* that might here have been discussed (see Chapter 1).

CHAPTER SIX

TOWARDS A BROADER CONSENSUS?

Yet all that has been said before in a didactic spirit does not gainsay one urgent imperative. It is simply that more of a consensus on defence policy needs to be sought within the West than recent years have seen. Potentially the most compelling of several good reasons is that, were we ever to face the imminent prospect of a major military reverse in, say, Europe or the lower Gulf or maybe even a strategic *bouleversement* across the world at large, too stark a polarisation of attitudes throughout the Atlantic community might not merely invite aggression. It could also cause responses to it at official level to become peculiarly erratic. Needless to say, the same could also apply in other countries (one thinks most readily of Australia and New Zealand, Israel, South Korea and Japan) which have close strategic ties with the United States and other Atlantic nations. If so, the actual policies pursued in a crisis might then gyrate in a dangerous fashion between supine appeasement, brittle intransigence and reckless over-reaction. Consider, for instance, the effect in 1940 of the political cleavages that were so tormenting France. That May, she was to exhibit a veritable paralysis of will in the face of a *blitzkrieg* against her own territory. Yet only a few weeks earlier, the then authorities in Paris had sought to stand taller than they inwardly felt by preparing (with grudging British connivance) armed intervention against the USSR in Finland. Mercifully, Helsinki's suing for peace with Moscow aborted what could only have been a catastrophe at every level.

Nor should one be exercised simply about contingent crises.

Even in much more normal circumstances, the proper examination of many other issues of direct or general relevance to the security of the NATO alliance and of the world at large continually get crowded out by endless declamations about 'the Bomb'. Yet in the defence field alone, a lot may depend on how some subtle balances are struck between deterrence or defence; deterrence or *detente*; defence or arms control; disarmament or arms control; restraint or reaction; and emergent or established technology. Take, for instance, the debate still in progress, especially in parts of Western Europe, about the modernisation of Intermediate Nuclear Forces. This debate ought to be shaped considerably by judgements about force size; force configuration; dual-key control; collateral Soviet deployments; and the state of West-East diplomacy. Unfortunately, however, the dialectic within the West is currently far too skewed and primitive to allow much venting of such comparatively intricate thoughts. Look how the Soviet deployment in East Germany of the SS-22 rockets has gone virtually unremarked. Look, too, at the obtuse refusal of not just the militant Left but of a wide range of presumptively informed opinion to take the slightest account of NATO's commitment soon to complete the withdrawal of a good third of the 6,500 battlefield nuclear weapons it had retained in the European theatre ever since the Kennedy era. Yet from this unsavoury ambience emerge two conflicting propositions. The one is that a salient element in the case for building a broader consensus on defence is that this may help to arrest an alarming flight from fact and logic, a flight by no means confined to matters of war and peace. But the other is that this is in itself a major impediment to achieving a fresh meeting of minds.

Alas, to draw attention thus to the urgency and yet the difficulty of the said task is, in the judgment of Sir Anthony Farrar-Hockley and myself, to underline the futility of going for a 'no first use' declaration or operational intent as a 'quick fix' solution. It cannot resolve the ethical dilemmas undeniably posed by nuclear firepower for every religious denomination and every political movement. To be more categoric, it cannot resolve them for a single church or party. By the same token, it cannot do so for any country or alliance within or aligned with

91

the West. Indeed, the chief problem that presents itself, as one seeks to counter the lately rising demand for 'no first use', is the sheer diversity of the counter-arguments that may legitimately be adduced. So let it be made clear that my presentation here of a fairly full spread is not to concede the intrinsic insufficiency of any of them. In our view, they are all able to stand on their individual merits. All the same, one cannot but accept that the emotions that surround this subject are too intense to be reoriented by one particular line of argument, whether or not it be valid. Nowhere is emotional fixation more evident than in the popular notion that the operational use of one nuclear warhead anywhere is equivalent to the release of all of them everywhere. The individual instance is equivalent to the final manifestation. Singular is the same as plural. Everything is subsumed by that omnibus term, 'the Bomb'.

In the more simplistic renderings, this supposed equivalence can be refuted merely by reference to the tendency towards the proliferation of nuclear weapons to nations that do not currently possess them: a tendency that many 'unilateral nuclear disarmers' and 'no first users' are intensely, sometimes obsessively, conscious of. Nobody would presume to suggest that a nuclear exchange between, let us say, India and Pakistan or Israel and an Islamic consortium or Argentina and Brazil would automatically precipitate a global holocaust. So why assume that a selective use of nuclear weapons by the USA, in or near such a regional theatre as the Korean peninsula or 'Near East Major', would ineluctably lead to that dread outcome? Should one not acknowledge that, all else apart, the probability of it is drastically reduced by the stable MAD relationship between Moscow and Washington, a development in military affairs almost as novel and far-reaching as was the first nuclear release in 1945?

Not that anybody in his right mind is going to pretend that even a limited nuclear release aimed at conflict termination would not administer to all Mankind a shock of a sort not known since 1945, at least. Just one low-yield fission weapon exploded well above a deserted Polish forest would be enough for that. Obviously, too, such a nuclear showdown might degenerate, and this sooner rather than later, into a fast-acting equivalent of some of history's greater traumas: the depredations of Genghiz Khan, the Black Death, the Negro slave trade, the Irish potato famine, the Nazi concentration camps or the Stalinist purges. Human civilisation did survive these wounds (wholly or largely self-inflicted, as they successively were) but the scars therefrom endure.

What has to be remembered, however, is that appropriate control arrangements are bound to reduce such a risk markedly. What also has to be remembered is that a leadership in the Kremlin that made war in Germany or some other theatre clearly regarded as vital by the West would be doing something even Joseph Stalin never quite brought himself to do, Korea notwithstanding. In other words, it would be in that sense uglier than anything we have ever seen in Moscow yet. What is more, once such hostilies had broken out the atmosphere the world over would rapidly become much more ugly still, thereby forcing on us far grimmer choices between alternative evils than can adequately be comprehended in a situation of peace, even be it armed peace. That much, at any rate, can be predicted with sombre confidence.

Nor is anybody entitled to contribute more than a couple of sentences to the debate on 'no first use' without telling the rest of us where he or she stands apropos of the efficacy of nuclear deterrence. Something approaching 200 distinct wars, half of them with an active international dimension, are generally reckoned to have occurred since 1945. Yet fewer than ten have occurred in Europe, none of these being as between NATO and the Warsaw Pact. No matter that Europe was the main fount and chief locus of two world wars earlier this century. Nor that much the same applies to warfare in the previous 400 years. True, other factors have contributed to what is, for Europeans at least, an agreeable paradox. More prosperity, urbanisation, communication and so on throughout what used to be called the Balkans have started to answer various ethnic minority questions in the best way of all, that of generating an attitude of indifference to them on the part of those most directly concerned. There and elsewhere, too, the extent to which states are loosely bound together within multi-national institutions (NATO and the Warsaw Pact included) has served to suppress old rivalries. But one does not have to believe that deterrence pure and simple is a remedy for all time to perceive that the fact that contemporary Europe is so strangely peaceable owes something to its exhibiting the starkest and densest manifestation of the nuclear balance of terror to be found anywhere on Earth. Also to be remarked is that two most flagrant cases of Communist military aggression outside Europe have occurred in two territories (Korea and Afghanistan) from which American protection appeared to have been withdrawn.

What then of the thesis that deterrence against non-nuclear attack could henceforward rest on non-nuclear weaponry, this by virtue of the accelerating revolution in military science? Actually, that is not a thesis in any integrative sense. Rather it is an assortment of proposals for 'alternative defence', proposals almost invariably abstracted from the real world of geography and politics. This being so, it is impossible to formulate a critique that is at once suitably brief and adequately definitive. But first this must be said. Most of those who advocate 'alternative defence' are seeking to do more than free themselves and the rest of us from dependence on nuclear weapons. For they are also trying to relate new visions of security to whatever ones they have of an 'alternative society'. Meanwhile, they are also endeavouring to relate the demands that prolonged non-nuclear defence would make on social cohesion to their often indulgent attitude not just to legitimate dissent but to civil disobedience. Likewise, they are making some attempt to square the premium their remedy would place on martial ardour with their own dislike of the martial virtues. Nowhere, of course, is their antipathy more intense yet convoluted than apropos of what one could entitle the Private Benjamin syndrome. First you insist that, in the armed services, women must be trained and otherwise treated the same as men. Then you turn round and say this denies their womanhood. Among the milder examples of such discordance is that afforded by Just Defence, a British grouping that is broadly centre Left and zealously committed to 'no first use'. The keynote of its exposition is that 'Small is Beautiful'! Duly, it depicts a panoply of weapons that are not just 'non-nuclear' but 'non-provocative'.[1] It consists largely of light guided missiles, anti-tank and anti-aircraft. Conceivably, this simple mix might have some effect against a mass tank charge with aircraft in close support. Certainly, it would be useless against echelons of mobile artillery backing a coordinative infantry/armour advance across an extended front (see Chapter 3).

The pleas from more orthodox quarters for non-nuclear defence in Germany, albeit within essentially the existing NATO structure and working from something like mainstream premises about politics and military science, are rather more persuasive *a priori*. But they may still be considerably open to criticism on the cardinal issue of ensuring sustained defensive power in this electronic era. Their authors would do well to recognise that the 'nuclear threshold' is defined in terms of the number of days NATO could be expected to sustain a non-nuclear resistance to a heavy attack; and that the immediate question, giving the trend to much more dynamic war, is not whether to raise or even eliminate this threshold but how best to prevent its falling. Five days will be a long time by 1995, especially in the aftermath of a sudden and massive attack. They also ought at least to essay an explanation of how they would wage such a war on certain other fronts or, indeed, on several fronts at once. They ought to acknowledge as well that, so far as the top military and political leadership is concerned, parrying a major attack by the enemy may be less difficult than inducing within him a change of heart sufficient to bring him to accept a cease-fire and enter into negotiations. Perhaps they should bear in mind, too, that the West is going to find it harder to use tactical air power to offset in part its vulnerability on the ground.

Then there is the big background factor of the social and economic stress consequent on war – meaning, above all else, the early development of critical strains within the international monetary sytem. Alas, it does not take long to identify several reasons why this has been so neglected a subject. The most obvious is that few soldiers and none too many of our academic strategists were ever trained as economists. Another is that the Anglo-American tradition of strategy is not a continentalist 'total war' one. Accordingly, economics tends to be aired within it only episodically or incidentally. But French strategic thinkers, too, have lately been preoccupied with matters nuclear, this thanks to there being a national nuclear question. Furthermore, the economics schools of modern academe are not habituated to thinking about monetary management in time of war. Also they tend to be political liberals of a vaguely Keynesian hue and hence would be diposed to assume that 'no first use' is a self-evident good. Across the road from them, metaphorically speaking, are the international bankers. They, too, find states of beligerence hard to hypothesize about. Also the optimistic faith that is an integral, and no doubt essential, part of their professional ethos readily extends to that now overlarge burden of liquid international debt, including the largish fraction incurred by the Soviet bloc. After all, the banks themselves were centrally instrumental in generating this state of affairs during the seventies. To some extent, they were spurred on by governments anxious to see petro-dollars so recycled as to promote *détente* with the Soviet bloc. But they were impelled, too, by their own sanguineness and overweening sense of adventure. Then as usual, their contact with the world of military security was minimal.

Put all these influences together, and it is hardly surprising that this parameter in the strategic balance regularly gets ignored by analysts and planning staffs. However, the argument stands that, while the banking community could probably avert a crippling crisis for the first few days of a Limited World War, it would be lucky to do so much beyond that. Even during the Falklands campaign, indeed, some assessment had to be made of the ability of the Galtieri regime to use its foreign debt as a means of economic warfare against the West, perhaps in response to major military operations by Britain against the mainland or the European economic sanctions. Nor can it seriously be contended that a 'no first use' declaration is a worthwhile aim within the quest for arms control and phased disarmament. Since it would remove all nuclear underpinning, it would very like render unviable not just MBFRs but Nuclear Free Zones. After all, the latter might depend on the ultimate guarantee against violent transgressions afforded by long-range nuclear weapons set further back.

Besides which, a joint 'no first use' commitment could tend to legitimise non-nuclear war and could, additionally or alternatively, lack credibility unless associated with extensive changes in force structure along appropriate lines.

Moreover, it would in itself be much to the geostrategic advantage of the USSR and her allies, just as was the case with the declamations of 30 years or so ago in favour of the renunciation of all nuclear firepower ahead of any other cutbacks in military paraphernalia. So better it would be by far to persuade Moscow to transmute its offer of a 'no first use' agreement into one precluding the first use of force of whatever kind. To which one might add that herein, too, lies a good reason why adoption of 'no first use' would be unlikely, when it came to the crunch, to increase American resolve to underwrite the defence of Europe. Another is that the whole thrust and tenor of the 'no first use' presentation has been so narrowly 'Euro-centric' that its acceptance would sap the concern many Americans still feel to uphold Western Europe because it can be their senior partner in the formulation of a strategy for global security and smooth development. Still, it is sometimes suggested that the community of strategic commentators and decision-takers really has no choice on this issue. Supposedly, there is a 'secular' or long-term tide of reluctance within Western society to countenance nuclear recourse. Surely, however, no tide is flowing at all steadily in favour of that or very much else. What is to be observed is that, much as with other utopian or millenarian movements at other times and places, the radical Left goes through upsurge and decline on a fairly regular eight to ten year cycle. Witness the recession of Communism in Western Europe in the late forties, of opposition to German rearmament in the middle fifties, of first-wave CND barely a decade later, and of the New Left/counter-culture around 1970. The latest peak has been passing more slowly but that is visibly a consequence of the world economic recession.

What is more, even at the peak of a radical upsurge the immediate effect is chiefly to polarise opinion and hence to consolidate a clear majority in favour of the nuclear defence of the Atlantic community and its critical interests and responsibilities further afield. Even these last several years, the evidence throughout the Atlantic area is overwhelmingly that a rejection of nuclear dissuasion is a liability at the polling stations, no matter that it may enable you to generate more in the way of televisual protest. What does appear as a relatively insistent trend is an increasing distaste for preparing for a European war of any kind. In the fifties and early sixties, this stemmed largely from a hedonistic enthusiasm for a newfound affluence and economic security. These last ten years, it has owed more to competing public priorities in an age of diminished economic growth, mounting unemployment and ageing populations. Undoubtedly, too, it has owed not a little to the residual influence of the counter-culture.

However, this proffers little comfort to the 'no first use' school. Take just the fiscal aspect. Not much has been said in this study about the economics of defence because the detailed costing long-term of various modes of non-nuclear defence is (a) a rather esoteric task, and (b) is dependent on some arbitrary assumptions about the nature of future war. But it is a matter of the most elementary logic that a mode that is not supported by preparations for nuclear recourse quite early on will always cost more than the same one that is backed up thus. Nor does one have to tarry long over arguments that nuclear release is unacceptable under international law because it is potentially a means of 'mass destruction'. First of all, such warheads could be used quite extensively without effecting mass destruction. All would depend on yield and targetting and whether ground bursting (which produces heavier fall-out) was taking place. Secondly, it may not be unfair to observe that those who stand on the principle of legality when hypothesising about this extreme situation are not always motivated as strongly over actual infringements of it of the sort alluded to in Chapter 5.

Lastly, a war between the major powers would today represent such a denial of the 'one world' precept that a whole corpus of legal and institutional arrangements would have to be suspended for the duration of hostilities. To suggest otherwise would be equivalent to saying, for instance, that even if one was satisfied (as some of us are) that the Anglo-American bomber offensive against the Third Reich was essential to the defeat of that regime, one would still have to condemn, as illegal in terms of pre-existing international law, the launching thus of a campaign of 'mass destruction'. But to do so would be to adopt the morality of the recluse. On the other hand, there are those who would aver that the initiation of a nuclear exchange is unconditionally unacceptable for reasons more fundamental than legal proprieties. They would focus on the possible extent of the cumulative devastation and on such strange and sinister effect as genetic damage to generations yet unborn. They would say, in effect, that 'All regimes depart but a nuclear calamity could prove irreparable. So better red than dead'.

Alas, there has been nothing in relations between the USSR and China; Vietnam and China; Vietnam and Cambodia; Yugoslavia and her neighbours; or the USSR and Eastern Europe to indicate that an Earth covered by Marxist-Leninist states would be one free from the curse of warfare. On the contrary, it could be more prone to go to war, nuclear included. After all, a signal respect in which Karl Marx's prevision has proved utterly wrong is the supposedly ineluctable withering away of socialist state systems, the eventual outcome being a blissful anarchy in which everybody collaborates freely with everybody else for ever more. Instead, those systems have proved exceptionally entrenched: centralised, secretive, cantankerous and martial.[2] Not to weigh this consideration when assessing one's moral obligations would again be to adopt the ethical stance not of the statesman but of the hermit. In short, it is very hard to think of a precept in the whole history of military science that has lain so open to such a battery of crippling objections as 'no first use' does. Nor should anybody make light of the responsibility assumed in seeking so fundamental a policy switch on the part of NATO and the other instruments of collective security through collective deterrence. For once accepted, transnational accords of this sort are liable to remain unchanged for a long time. After all, 'flexible response' has survived over twenty years as *de facto* NATO strategy and nearly as long *de jure*. A precept which, like 'no first use', was supposed to represent a singular moral stance might prove even more enduring, almost irrespective of changes in the objective situation. Therefore, it is incumbent on those who espouse it to marshal counter-arguments of the greatest comprehension, candour and cogency. Thus far, however, their approach has been cavalier to the point of flippancy. Two examples may suffice, one from Britain and the other from the USA.

On 10 February 1983, the General Synod of the Church of England debated the *Church and the Bomb* report mentioned in Chapter 2. After what does appear to have been a civilised and serious discussion, it rejected the essentially unilateralist position of the said study by 338 to 100. Then late that day a follow-up motion was introduced which made a plea for a general reduction of nuclear weapons on all sides. But then, Bishop Hugh Montefiore of Birmingham urgently moved an amendment seeking to repudiate 'first use' in any circumstances. He said it was 'not defence but naked aggression' and that the aim of so inherently 'evil' a pitch was 'deliberately to loose hell on Earth'. With little further ado, Synod approved his amendment by 275 votes to 222, while referring it to discussion in the dioceses. One cannot but protest that so crucial a topic was handled so clumsily and as not much more than 'any other business', an afterthought intended to console the unilateralists.

The other instance is even less acceptable because it was the product of more calculated consideration. In an article published in 1983, Robert McNamara opined that 'nuclear weapons serve no military purpose whatsoever. They are totally useless – except only to deter one's opponent from using them. This is my view. It was my view in the early 1960s.'[3] Alas, Mr McNamara has to be reminded that, as US Secretary of Defense from 1961, he masterminded more than did any other individual the massive build-up of tactical nuclear warheads in NATO Europe in 'the early 1960s', a build-up that effectively was to provide the alliance with its inventory in that sphere for the next two decades. One has to reiterate, too, that this inventory has been not just large but very diverse and well distributed, as witness the total of well over 2,000 nuclear shells for various types of artillery gun. It all represents, in fact, liberal provision for that first contingent and 'flexible' use of nuclear weapons that Mr McNamara was so actively endorsing from 1962. In just the same way, the US expansion of strategic forces during this time owes a lot to most liberal allowance being made for the waging of Limited Strategic War. Herein was a set of options that Mr McNamara himself articulated with some enthusiasm, notably as part of his speech at Ann Arbor that June (see Chapter 2) and in one in Chicago that January.

All the same, the quest for a wider consensus on matters appertaining to defence must go on and must be dynamic. We cannot merely wait for the mainstream forces of the political centre and Right to fill the political vacuum which presumably will remain as, once again, the 'peace movement' goes into cyclical decline. For one thing, every such phase leaves some legacy. For another, cyclical movements by definition alternate. So, were its aspirations to go entirely unrequited, a militant challenge from the Left would be almost bound to resurge within a decade, perhaps in world and European circumstances yet harsher and less stable than those we currently experience. However, the plain fact is that divergences over defence are largely reflections of deeper divisions in our society: divisions caused and sustained by economic, social and, to an ever-increasing extent, ecological stress. In other words, we will not secure a wide enough consensus on 'nuclear first use' until we start to sort ourselves out on structural unemployment, urban decay, alienation in the work place, cultural deprivation, participatory democracy and environmental pollution. The tragic irony is that many of these problems, not least the environmental ones, also make a manifold impact on the prospects for long-term peace. The tragedy and the irony are compounded by there being many on the moderate Left who could make a good contribution to dealing with them but are currently directing their energies chiefly to 'unilateralism' or 'no first use'. This is in part because these nostra have made less demands on their intellectual stamina in that they appear to be less immediately operational. It is also in part because the ethical alternatives can be posited as simple to the point of banality.

So one has to insist that the alternatives are not that simple and that operational crises are always liable to break at alarmingly short notice. What one can aver as well is that, in the sphere of Defence as such, other themes wait to be explored, themes which, though they would never hold any interest to the fascisto-Marxist extremists within what is pleased to dignify itself as the 'peace movement', ought to attract that larger proportion which is still concerned somehow to preserve Western society as such. One is that Mutual Assured Destruction as between Moscow and Washington is an excellent basis from which to explore more urgently the limitation of strategic arms.[4] Obversely, the electronic revolution is going to invite big changes in the configuration of local war forces and hence of the professional mores of those who serve in them. Not to generate a wider debate on this broad subject may be to allow these changes to be distorted and stultified by bureaucratic politics altogether too much. It may, in particular, be to preclude our future force posture being sufficiently well adapted to what must be the longer term haul to the limitation and control of armaments at theatre level. So for all concerned now to consume precious months and years either advocating or refuting 'no first use' would be a diversion disastrous beyond belief. It would undercut all more constructive enquiry, including any along the lines just adumbrated but including, too, the reconsideration so long overdue of the modalities of nuclear control. A key aspect of the latter is, of course, the demonstrative use of nuclear firepower (perhaps preceded by non-nuclear strikes with precision-guided munitions) in some sector that stands apart from the main battle area. That may not be conducive to threshold raising as such but it is to proper civil-military control; and it may, in fact, be the best way to initiate crisis termination through nuclear interruption. To which must be added that a lot more attention ought to be paid to the whole question of civil-military relationships, at every level, during a warlike crisis. So ought it to the formulation of a comprehensive strategy (military, political, economic and ecological) for global stability and peace.[5]

What is more, were 'no first use' ever to be made the

foundation of our military doctrine, it could all too readily prove tantamount to a strategy of pre-emptive surrender. Accordingly, it could set off a chain of events whereby nuclear warfare (and perhaps, in the ultimate, a Marxist-Leninist nuclear winter) became a stronger possibility than ever before.

NOTES AND REFERENCES

PART II

Nuclear First Use – An Overview

1   DETERRENCE IN EUROPE

1 Neville Brown 'The Security Question in Central Europe' *ADIU Report* vol 5, no 5, September/October 1983 pp.1-4.
2 David Rees, *Korea – The Limited War* (Macmillan, London, 1964), Chapter 22.
3 Edward Jay Epstein *Harpers*, vol 267, no 1802, November 1983 p. 48.
4 See e.g. Michael Carver, *A Policy for Peace* (Faber and Faber, London, 1982).
5 See Neville Brown, *Limited World War?* (The Australian National University, Canberra, 1985), Chapter 2.
6 *Ibid* Chapters 1 and 5.

2   THE CONTROL OF ESCALATION

1 This examination is largely derived from Neville Brown 'The Future of the British Deterrent. 1. The Use of Nuclear Weapons', *Navy International*, vol 88, no 4, April 1983, pp. 240-244.
2 *The Church and the Bomb* (Hodder and Stoughton, London, 1982). The working party was headed by Bishop John Baker of Salisbury.
3 An extract from the virtually identical memoranda sent by France, in March 1966, to each of her NATO allies. This was to advise them of her impending withdrawal from NATO's military commands.
4 Reprinted, in English translation, in *Survival*, Vol 18 (5), September/October, 1976, pp. 228-230.

5 André Beaufre 'The Sharing of Nuclear Responsibilities: A Problem in need of Solution', *International Affairs*, vol. XXXI, no 3, July 1965, p. 416.

3   THE CHANGING FACE OF WAR

1 See Neville Brown *An Unbreakable Nuclear Stalemate* (The Council for Arms Control, London, 1982) p. 5.
2 Carl Sagan 'Nuclear War and Climatic Catastrophe: Some Policy Implications', *Foreign Affairs*, vol 62, no 2, Winter 1983/4 pp. 257-92.
3 For some further development of the technical arguments, see Neville Brown's paper 'Lethal Beams in Space' presented to the 6th National Quantum Electronics Conference at the University of Sussex in September 1983. This paper is reproduced in *Navy International*, vol 88 no 11, November 1983, pp. 676-681.
4 'Soviets Test New Cruise Missiles', *Aviation Week and Space Technology*, vol 120, no 1, January 1984 pp. 14-16.
5 FM-100-5 *Operations* (Department of the Army, Washington DC, 1976), Chapter 2, paragraph 2.
6 *Ibid*, Chapter 2, paragraph 23.
7 B.H. Liddell Hart *Deterrent or Defence* (Stevens and Co, London, 1960), Chapters 10 and 12.
8 B.H. Liddell Hart 'The Ratio of Troops to Space', *The RUSI Journal* vol CV, no 618, May 1960, pp. 201-212.
9 See Neville Brown 'The Changing Face of Non-Nuclear War', *Survival*, vol XXIV, no 5, September/October 1982, pp. 211-219.
10 F.W. Lanchester *Aircraft in Warfare: the Dawn of the Fourth Arm* (Constable, London, 1916), p. 26.
11 Mach 1·0 is the speed of sound at the altitude in question. At sea level, it is circa 760 m.p.h.
12 See Professor Brown's Inaugural Lecture *Silver Wings in the Twilight* (University of Birmingham, Birmingham, 1983), p. 8.
13 'The Changing Face of Non-Nuclear War' op. cit, pp. 218-219.
14 See Alva Myrdal *The Game of Disarmament* (Manchester University Press, Manchester, 1977).

4   THE CENTRAL EUROPEAN THEATRE

1 A megaton is an explosive potential equivalent to a million tons of TNT. A kiloton corresponds to a thousand. The figure of 1,250 is derived mainly from Robert S. McNamara, 'The Military Role of Nuclear Weapons', *Foreign Affairs*, vol 62, no 1, Fall 1983, pp. 59-80.

2 See e.g. *The Report of the Subcommittee on Defence Cooperation On The Implications of Technology for the Battlefield* (The North Atlantic Assembly, Paris, 1982), pp. 1-7.
3 *The Guardian*, 14 November 1961.
4 *The Military Balance, 1983-84*, (The International Institute for Strategic Studies, London, 1983), pp. 3 – 42.
5 Neville Brown 'Air Power in Central Europe', *The World Today*, vol 39, no 10, October 1983, pp.378-384.
6 R.L. Fischer, Adelphi Paper No 127, *Defending the Central Front: The Balance of Forces* (International Institute for Strategic Studies, London, 1976), p. 33.
7 Richard Lawrence and Jeffrey Record, *US Force Structure in NATO* (The Brookings Institution, Washington DC, 1974), p. 44.
8 *NATO and the Warsaw Pact. Force Comparisons* (NATO Information Service, Brussels, 1984), Figure 2.

5   THE WIDER COMPASS

1 *Limited World War?* (The Australian National University, Canberra, 1985), Chapter 3.
2 'Mission Imperative', *Armed Forces*, August 1983, pp. 304-8.
3 *The Military Balance, 1983-4, op. cit*, pp. 16, 54 and 55.
4 Neville Brown, *Strategic Mobility* (Chatto and Windus for Institute for Strategic Studies, London, 1963), Chapter 2.
5 *The Economist*, 21 January 1984.
6 S.E. Johnson and J.A. Yager, *The Military Equation in Northeast Asia.* (The Brookings Institution, Washington DC, 1979), p. 47.
7 Sir Anthony Farrar-Hockley 'Dynamic Defence: the Northern Flank', *RUSI Journal*, vol 128, no 4, December 1983, pp. 5-11.

6   TOWARDS A BROADER CONSENSUS?

1 Frank Barnaby and Stan Windass *What is Just Defence?* (Just Defence, Oxford, 1983), pp. 3 and 8.
2 See the author's 'The Delusions of Neutralism', *RUSI Journal*, vol 126, no 3, September 1981, pp. 27-33.
3 'The Military Role of Nuclear Weapons', *Foreign Affairs*, vol 62, no 1, Fall 1983, pp. 59-60.
4 See Neville Brown 'A Consensus On MAD', *ADIU Report*, vol 6, no 2, March/April 1984, pp. 1-4.
5 See the author's Chapter 5 in Josephine O'Connor-Howe (Ed.), *Armed Peace – The Search for World Security* (Macmillan for Council for Arms Control, London, 1984).

INDEX

Afghanistan, invasion of, 34-35, 84, 94

Arms control, 23, 27, 47, 57, 91, 96-97, 102

Artillery guns, 17-18, 60, 62-63, 66-68, 71, 75-76, 78, 95, 100

Atlantic Alliance, 11, 15, 18, 33, 40, 48-49, 58, 90-92, 100

Ballistic Missile Defence (BMD), 47, 55-57, 70

Berlin, West, 28, 35, 49

Britain, 17-18, 39-41, 46, 53, 73-74, 79, 96, 100

Canada, 15, 33, 77-78, 81

Chemical weapons, 14-16, 26, 35, 37, 41, 43, 50-51, 74, 77

China, 27, 29, 84

Christian reactions, 24, 43, 100

Clausewitz, Karl von, 42, 75

Command and control, 12-14, 17, 35, 37, 40, 44-47, 49-50, 55, 57, 67, 70-71, 81, 93, 102

Conscription, 64, 69-70, 72, 78

Cuba crisis, 58, 76

Détente, 37, 91, 96

Deterrence, 23-24, 27, 35, 47-48, 50-51, 71, 91, 93-94, 99

'Domino theory', Soviet, 34, 82

Escalation, 29, 37, 38-52, 57, 75, 83, 86, 88, 92 (see also Limited Strategic War, Limited World War etc.)

Fascisto-Marxism, 29, 33, 63-64, 89, 97, 102

Flexible response, 39-40, 74-75, 92, 99

France, 13, 17-18, 39-41, 44-47, 53, 73, 77-79, 90, 96

Germany, West and East, 18, 28-29, 35-36, 60, 73-75, 77, 80-81, 91, 95

Ground-Launched Cruise Missiles (GLCM), BGM-109A, 73

Gulf theatre, 35, 48, 83-87

Helicopters, 61, 68

Infantry, 61-62, 95

Intermediate-range Nuclear Forces (INF), 46, 58, 73-74, 76-77, 91

International monetary instability, 30-33, 36-37, 50, 84, 95-96

Israel, 28, 48, 61, 68-69, 82, 84, 90, 92, 95-96

Italy, 18, 74

Japan, 28, 50-51, 70, 84, 87, 90

Korea, North and South, 28, 37, 48, 61, 83, 87-89, 90

Korean War, 12-13, 29, 87-88, 94

Lanchester, F.W., 62-63, 68

Liddell Hart, Sir Basil, 61-62, 64
Limited Strategic War, 40, 43-44, 58, 76-77, 85-86, 101
Limited World War, 35-37, 48-50, 58-59, 96
Low Countries, 74, 78

McNamara, Robert, 25, 41, 73-74, 100-101
Martial ethos, 27, 64, 70, 72, 94-95, 102
Mines, 17, 25, 37, 60
Mutual Assured Destruction (MAD), 53-58, 92, 102
Mutual and Balanced Force Reductions (MBFRs), 27-28, 96

North Atlantic Treaty Organisation (NATO), 11-19, 23-24, 26-30, 33, 62, 73-79, 93, 95, 99-100
NATO Scandinavia, 28, 35, 48, 78, 89
'Near East Major', 34-35, 37, 48-49, 84-86
'No early use', 12, 23, 26-27, 33, 35, 48-49, 59, 72, 88-89, 92, 97-98, 102-103
Nuclear doctrine, Soviet, 15-17, 42-44
Nuclear threshold, 14-18, 24, 35-36, 69, 95
Nuclear weapons, strategic, 14, 24, 40, 51-55, 76, 80, 89
Nuclear weapons, tactical, 17-18, 24, 45, 73-76, 88-89, 91, 100-101
'Nuclear winter', 54-55, 103

Palestinian Arabs, 84
Pershing missiles, 73

Radical Left, 33, 85, 97, 101

Radical Right, 33
Reinforcement, 26-27, 37, 49, 63, 65, 71, 78-81, 86
Replenishment, 14, 26, 49, 63, 65, 71

Satellites in orbit, 48, 67 (see also Ballistic Missile Defence)
South Africa, 28, 32
Soviet bloc, 29-30, 32-34, 47, 69-70, 76, 82, 96-97, 99
Submarines, 17, 29-30, 41, 43-44, 53-54, 83, 89
Surprise attack, 12-14, 26, 37, 47, 49, 64, 67-68, 75

Tactical aviation, 49, 60, 64-70, 73-76, 78-81, 86, 95
Tanks, 25, 59, 61, 64, 66, 78, 95
Turkey, 28, 48-49, 61, 84

Unilateralist 'peace movement', 24, 36, 38-39, 83, 97, 101-102
Union of Soviet Socialist Republics (USSR), 11-12, 15-18, 25, 34-35, 42-44, 47, 57-58, 69-70, 76-79, 84, 90, 97, 99
United States of America (USA), 11, 15, 17, 24-25, 27, 29, 39, 47, 53-58, 73-74, 78-79, 81, 84, 90, 100-101

Warsaw Pact, 12-14, 17-18, 23-26, 44, 49, 53-58, 75-81, 93
World War One, 31, 63, 93
World War Two, 25-26, 31, 50-51, 53-54, 65-66, 72, 73, 90, 93, 97, 98-99

'Yom Kippur' war, 13, 68